GARIFUNA
TRAVEL JOURNEY

LABUGA – LIVINGSTON

Lucia Cayetano Guity

DEDICATION

I dedicate this book to the memory of my father, Mr Inocente Cayetano, who passed away at age 71. And my mother Mrs Froilana Sandoval De Cayetano. My memory of her is her beautiful smile. She passed away at age 82. For their unconditional love for me and protectiveness in raising me until the age of 27 when my father had the honor to walk me down the aisle in the St. Martin de Porres Church feeling proud. I also dedicate this book to my late husband of 36 years of marriage, Edward Edgar Guity, also known as Juni Guity Vargas, for his devotion to our love and marriage and for being an example Father. He is my eternal love.

I want to express my gratitude to my only son, Edward A. Guity Jr., A Navy veteran. His service to the USA of America is that of loyalty and bravery. I thank him for his service. I am a very proud Mom. Thank you for making me a Navy Mom. God bless you.

I extend my dedication to my supporters, Mr. Roy Cayetano and Mr. Ruben C. Guity. They have been the voice of reason to me when I needed to talk to someone. *Thank you* for your guidance.

PREFACE

In the mosaic of life, each piece is infused with stories of journeys, struggles, and triumphs. My story is a vibrant element in the rich mosaic of the Garifuna culture—a narrative that spans continents, cultures, and generations. It begins in the landscapes of Livingston, a small coastal town in Guatemala, where I was born and where the Caribbean Sea meets the emerald waters of the Rio Dulce.

As the youngest child of a family deeply rooted in Garifuna traditions, I grew up in a world where migration was a generational survival pattern, an echo of our ancestral exile from St. Vincent isle of the Greater Antilles. The rhythm of the sea shaped my early years, the tastes of American treats mixed with our local flavors, and the warmth of a community where everyone was, in some way, family. This environment—immersed in the principles and values passed down through generations—shaped not just how I saw the world but also how I moved through it.

Our journeys took us further than the ferry rides between Puerto Barrios and Livingston. When my father retired from the American Fruit Company, we moved to the United States. As a child, I had no say in this migration. It was another chapter in our family's narrative of movement and adaptation, mirroring the migrations that defined my ancestors' lives. In

America, my path led me to pursue higher education and a career that allowed me to write extensively, crafting psycho-social assessments that required empathy, understanding, and an ability to connect with others across differences—a skill undoubtedly honed by my upbringing.

This book is more than a recollection of memories; it is an invitation to journey with me through the landscapes of my life, both geographical and emotional. It is a reflection on how the values and principles of the Garifuna culture have guided me to maneuver the complexities of modern life and how these guiding stars have helped me balance between the worlds I inhabit, serving as beacons in my life.

As a retired Garifuna woman, writing has become my bridge between the past and the future. It is my hope that these pages will inspire others, offering insights into the importance of maintaining one's cultural identity while embracing the changes that life invariably brings. In sharing my story, I aim to contribute to the collective memory of my people and to enrich the understanding of all who walk into the world of the Garifuna.

This is not just my journey; it is a testament to the enduring spirit of a people who have navigated through adversity with resilience and grace. Welcome to the story of my life—a narrative forged in the fires of experience and cooled in the waters of reflection.

TABLE OF CONTENTS

Chapter 1
Garifuna

Nestled along the vibrant Caribbean coast, where the lavish tropical rainforests of Central America meet the vast azure waters, lies the soulful town of Livingston. This strategic location has made Livingston an important port town, bustling with merchant ships. Known as *La Buga* to the Garifuna people. It is a place where different cultures mix together, reflecting the resilience and spirit of a community that has prospered despite all the challenges.

The town is named after Edward Livingston, a North American legislator known for his work on the penal system. This connection was detailed by Tito Basi in his book *"Livingston Forever,"* where he describes how the Guatemalan country adopted the name during Livingston's time as the political head of Izabal.

Throughout its history, Livingston has been a hub for trade, with ships arriving to load up on local products like coconuts, pineapples, bananas, and coffee from the highlands of Altaverapaz. These goods were then shipped off to markets in the United States and Europe. Today, the port remains active, now also dealing with industrial materials and tourists.

Livingston's history is deeply connected to its founder, Marcos Sanchez Diaz, whom the people of this town honor as a founder and protector of their land. As noted by Alfonso Arrillaga Cortez in his book *"Marcos Sanchez Diaz,"* Marcos played a crucial role in establishing the community by clearing land and setting up villages. Families like the *Castillo, Avila, Cayetano, Sambula, Palacios, and Martinez,* as mentioned in the book, are considered foundational to the Garifuna community.

Marcos Sanchez Diaz was not just a community leader; he was seen as a Huayba—a chief or indigenes prince during the Spanish Colonial Era. With compassion, he assisted the Garifuna, displaced from St. Vincent, in finding a new home in Roatan, an island off main land Honduras that was occupied by the Spaniards. However, the island was too small to sustain them, leading Marcos to guide the Black Carib to other coastal areas in the Caribbean suitable for their new settlements.

Livingston is a lively hub where ancient traditions are kept alive regardless of the influences of the modern world.

The Garifuna, an Afro-Indigenous people, trace their origins back to the early 17th century on the island of St. Vincent. The mixture of Africans who escaped two shipwrecked Spanish ships and the local Carib and Arawak populations birthed a unique culture, one that fiercely resisted European colonization. However, in the late 18th century, after continued conflict and the death of their leader, Joseph Satuyer, the British exiled the Garifuna to Roatán, an island off the coast of Honduras. From there, they spread along the coastlines of Belize, Guatemala, Nicaragua, and Honduras.

Joseph Chatoyer was their first chief, who was also a fierce defender and skilled negotiator during the turbulent times of the 1760s and beyond. When the French and the British were vying for control, with the British eager to take over the fertile lands that the Black Caribs had inhabited, it was Chatoyer who stood firm. He led his people through many battles, and in 1773, his efforts resulted in a peace agreement with the British, clearly marking the lands where his people could live safely.

However, peace was short-lived. By 1795, tensions rose again, and Chatoyer led a rebellion against British encroachment. Despite initial successes, the British, under General Ralph Abercromby, eventually overpowered the Caribs. The aftermath was grim: in 1796, over 5,000 of his people were deported to Roatán, an island off Honduras. Tragically, only about 2,500 survived the harsh journey. Those who managed to establish a life spread across Central America, evolving into what they now proudly call the *Garifuna*.

Livingston, the cultural town in Guatemala, represents one of these significant settlements. This town which is accessible only by *boat*, serves not just as a geographical location but as a spiritual heartland for the Garifuna. It is here that the Rio Dulce, known for its bright green waters and warm springs, drains into the Caribbean Sea, creating a vivid symbol of the Garifuna journey—flowing persistently and resiliently towards open waters.

The Garifuna culture clearly demonstrates their continuing spirit and history of overcoming challenges. The culture is a vibrant showcase of unique traditions covering music, dance, and culinary practices, which have been artfully depicted in the works of Garifuna authors like a Garifuna Duchess in her memoir *"Spiritual Journey"* and Tito Basi in *"Livingston Forever."*

Punta is a famous tradition of the Garifuna people, a music with a fast beat played on drums. People dance in a sensual way to this music, a fun way for the Garifuna people to remember their history and celebrate their strong spirits. These rhythmic sounds connect the Garifuna to their ancestors and show how their culture has survived over time.

The Garifuna people have a special way of speaking, like a mix of different languages. Their words come from Arawakan (like their ancestors spoke), Carib (from people they met on their journey), and African dialect from West Africa, adding a layer of vocabulary that reflects their shared experiences, French (from colonists), and even English, a testament to the ever-evolving nature of language. This unique blend is more than just words; it's evidence of their enduring spirit and a vibrant reminder of their history. Their unwavering commitment to preserving their unique identity shines through in every word they speak.

When I met Mrs. Salome Cayetano, an elder in Dangriga, Belize, she told me something I'll never forget. She said, "You are one of our own. All Cayetanos around here are family." The

Garifuna, she explained, always settle where rivers flow into the sea. This helps them thrive. The women grow their food like yams, cassava, plantains, and okra upriver in the highlands. The male went out for fishing in the sea. They returned with tones of sea food. The villagers welcomed them and everyone got their share to feed their families.

Festivities play a crucial role in Garifuna culture, with the annual celebration of Garifuna Settlement Day on November 19th being a pinnacle event. This day honors their arrival in Central America with parades, live music, dancing, and traditional meals like *hudut,* which is a savory fish coconut stew seasoned with garlic, basil, onion, and peppers. Then there's Alabundiga, made from grated green bananas cooked gently in coconut milk to keep their shape, and sometimes fish is added. It reminds them of the food from both the land and the ocean!

Garifuna food is another big part of their culture which offers a delicious trip through their history and its adaptations from different ethnicities. Dishes such as *cassava bread*, an essential in the Garifuna diet, connect back to the indigenous roots of the Arawak and Carib. Cassava is poisonous if untreated, but the Garifuna figured out a special way to turn it into a decadent delight and filling bread. It undergoes a labor-intensive transformation into a nourishing and versatile bread, symbolizing the Garifuna's ability to adapt and thrive in harsh conditions. Making cassava bread is a social event, especially for women. The grandmas teach the younger girls how to make it, sharing not only cooking skills but also stories about their heritage. So, every bite of this bread is like a taste of Garifuna's history and culture!

Rice and beans are another Garifuna specialty. It's made with coconut milk, rice, and red pinto beans, served with fried fish or meat, and often enjoyed as a Sunday lunch. Growing up, everyone in the village had rice fields and breadfruit trees. If you didn't have breadfruit, you just asked a neighbor.

The use of seafood and coconut in Garifuna cooking not only highlights their connection to the sea but also showcases the blending of natural resources from their environment into their daily sustenance. Fish, conch, and shrimp prepared with coconut milk and spices reflect a palette that is as diverse as the Garifuna people themselves.

Garifuna's values are deeply embedded in the community. Their spirituality is deeply rooted in their history with the Catholic Church, introduced by Jesuits and other missionaries. Yet, it's blended with their unique beliefs and practices that honor their ancestors and the supreme being, known as *Bungiu* or *Sunti Gabafu* (All-Powerful). The spiritual leader in their communities, known as the *Buyei*, guides all their traditional practices, ensuring that they maintain a deep connection with their past and the spiritual world.

One of their most profound practices is the *Dugu* ceremony, a mystical event that heals and restores balance within their community. It's a time when they come together to honor their obligations to the spirits of their ancestors through food, prayer, and song, which helps ensure their support and guidance in their daily lives. This shared relationship with their ancestors is fundamental to their way of life, influencing everything from their health to community decisions.

They also have deep respect for nature and believe their ancestors are always watching over them. Their spirituality is a blend of African animist beliefs, Carib and Arawak traditions, and Christian elements, exemplified in the Dugu ceremony. If they neglect these spiritual duties, the ancestors make their needs known through dreams, prompting them to organize a *Dugu*. This ritual serves as a means to heal and restore balance within the community through offerings, drumming, and dance, invoking the guidance of ancestors to resolve communal conflicts or illnesses, their way of getting back in balance and staying strong as a community.

In Livingston, the daily life of a Garifuna extends beyond mere survival. It is an ongoing celebration of their heritage, a continual reclamation of their identity in the modern world.

Imagine a giant family reunion that never ends; that's the essence of Livingston. Here, the heart of the community beats at the *gulisi*, a special open-air space that serves as a town hall, a social hub, and sometimes even a dance floor. Beneath the shade of swaying palm trees, villagers of all ages gather. Here, decisions are made, stories are shared, and disputes are settled. The elders play a crucial role, not just as keepers of wisdom but as active participants in the governance and social well-being of their community. They ensure that the traditions and lessons from the past are not lost but are instead entwined into the community's evolving narrative.

Evenings in Livingston are a sensory feast. As the sun sets, the air fills with the rhythmic beat of drums from the *gulisi*. Young men showcase their expertise in drumming circles, the pulse of the music resonating the heartbeat of the community. Women adorned with brightly colored fabrics gracefully swaying to the music. The aroma of freshly grilled fish floats from open-air kitchens, mingling with the scent of woodsmoke from cooking fires. Sharing stories, laughter, and a delicious meal under the starlit sky – *pure joy.*

Education and the passing on of knowledge occur in informal settings, where the elders teach the young about their rights and responsibilities through stories and daily tasks. This method of learning helps preserve the Garifuna language and cultural practices in a world where formal education often prioritizes Western methods and languages. It is through these communal interactions that the Garifuna children learn the importance of their cultural identity and help retain its essence.

As the youngest child of a Garifuna watchman who journeyed from watching over the fruit-laden vessels at sea to painting ships and finally opening a store in Puerto Barrios, I have lived through the transformation of our community. From my earliest days in Barrio Barrique, where the elite of our village established their homes, to the bustling, dusty roads of Puerto Barrios, and eventually, to the diverse landscapes of the United States, I have carried with me the lessons of my people—their tenacity, their joy, and their unparalleled ability to adapt and thrive.

The tale of my life, laid out on these pages, is both an homage to the past and a guidepost for the future. The saga of my life, which began in 1980...

Chapter 2

Early Days Till Departure

Never before had a song felt so much like a memory of my arrival in this world, in my beautiful village. A special song called *"Las Mañanitas"* or darling morning dew, that's often sung to celebrate birthdays. It goes like this:

On the day you were born,
All the flowers bloomed,
And the birds sang beautiful songs.
Wake up, little darling, wake up,
Because the moon will soon be gone.

This song has lived in my mind for years whenever I recall my precious memories to cherish the time I spent in Livingston. It reminds me of my own beginning.

I was born early on a Tuesday morning at 4:30 am, on June 25th, 1956. It was a beautiful day in my little village of Barrio Barrique in Labuga Livingston, Guatemala. The Caribbean Sea sent a cool breeze that morning, making everything seem peaceful. My brave mother, Froilana, and my father, Inocente Cayetano, were there, along with my six siblings and the village midwife, the Dula. They all welcomed me, the seventh child, into the world. They say seven is God's number—maybe that's why I've always felt lucky.

Growing up in Barrio Barrique was like living in a tropical paradise. I cherish those memories deeply. The whole village celebrated when I arrived, but according to Garifuna traditions, no one outside the immediate family could see me until I was three months old. During that time, my mother was looked after by her cousins and my older siblings. I remember her telling me stories about my infant days. The midwife was always there, helping bathe me with sacred herbs and chamomile. Every part of me was cared for tenderly, even my little mouth, which was cleansed with honey, and my entire little body was massaged with almond oil. A red string was tied on my right wrist to repel negative energies. Initially, I was breastfed until age two and a half. Thereafter, I was fed clear cassava porridge to nourish my growing body.

When I turned three months old, I was dressed in a beautiful white dress and taken to the only church in town, *Our Lady of Sacred Heart*. It was a big event, with the family and villagers filling up the church, singing and praying over me. That's when my father named me *Lucia*, which means light, but he always called me *Clara Luz*, meaning clear light. I love that name; it feels like it truly matches who I am, bringing light into darkness or beacon of light.

Lucia Cayetano Guity

My earliest memories start around when I was four or five years old, but they're a bit fuzzy. Being the youngest child, I was often called "*the youngest*" by everyone, and my father affectionately called me *Clara Luz*. I spent a lot of time just watching life go by, playing silently by myself next to our old dog, Motico, who was too old to see or run. Well, someone had him as a puppy. He became my hand-me-down dog. All I had to do was caress him and feel saddened for him. I would make mud clay plates and pretend to cook beside the house, feeling invisible and a bit lonely since my older siblings didn't really play with me as no one wanted to bother with a younger sibling. There were not many children my age to play with, so I was on my own.

One day, I found myself at a kindergarten school not far from our house. I don't recall any discussion of this plan. I was shy and felt out of place, but I enjoyed drawing and singing songs about little chicks. This was my first step into a bigger world, one where I could meet other children and learn new things. Well, my introduction to socialization and competition. The feeling was overwhelming for me as a young child yet exciting as I enjoyed singing and hopping like a bunny with the other children.

Life in Livingston was simple; we didn't have TVs, theaters, or playgrounds. Our playground was the bay, the sand, and the sea. We'd collect shells, swim among the seagrass, and later sit in a canoe under a coconut tree, enjoying the breeze. Every day was filled with these small adventures like these.

Part of my being acculturated to the Garifuna culture was to spend a lot of time with the elders. I remember going to the Arabu, our family farm, with my Aunt, Tia Wawa. We'd walk along the shore, crossing streams that flowed into the sea, picking sea grapes and mangoes along the way and devouring them. The memory of their round leaves magnetically facing the sea is unforgettable. The farm was a magical place for me, filled with yams, cassava, and rice. Aunt Tia Wawa would tell me stories about our ancestors and teach me about the plants and animals we encountered. She played a big part in my childhood, showing me the beauty of our land and the richness of our heritage.

Lucia Cayetano Guity

My imagination grew with the small details I observed as we continued to walk under the sun. I would leap and hop across another stream, where the water appeared reddish or oxidized. I also noticed a small crocodile at a distance; they are also known as caliman or alligators. Well, this one was just two feet long, so it didn't scare me much; I was just curious.

As we wandered around, this adventure kindled further as we approached mangrove vegetation in an area called Queweche. Auntie directed me to walk into the sea during low tide so that we could walk over the sand that was visible, avoiding the deep parts of the river. As we crossed, I noticed the roots of the mangroves clinging to the bottom of the water and round blue crabs crawling over their roots. My Aunt's farmhouse, our lodging on the farm, stands one hundred feet away from the river. It was a simple lodge used during farm stays, equipped with a wooden stove, dishes, pots, pans, and hammocks tied from one corner to another. The lodge, made of local wood and palm leaves for a rooftop, was cool and somewhat dark, providing a good shade from the sun.

Auntie washed the mullets we picked along the seashore, along with clams we dug out, crabs, and small colorful clams called suwindiri found buried in the sand. She rinsed everything and made a delicious soup called *tapow*—a mixture of seafood and vegetables like yams and cassava, flavored with basil she grew around her hut. I savored every bit of it.

After the meal, we rested because, the next day, we would go uphill to the farm. We lay on the hammocks, and she would tell me stories about how we arrived in Labuga Livingston and where we came from—a faraway place called *Yurumen*, or *St. Vincent*. "We are Arawak," she said. Aunt Tia Wawa had a significant impact on my childhood. Even though she was not my mother, she spent quality time with me. There's an African saying that it takes a village to raise a child. Her gentle voice, loving smile, and nurturing nature were an example of the spirit of the Arawak indigenous people.

During the morning, I was awakened by the sun's rays. I hopped off the hammock and walked a few yards towards the seashore that shimmered by the bright sun. The seawater was shallow and crystal clear, and refreshingly delightful. I chased the tiny sea crabs as they would playfully hide in the sand. This memory remains vividly in my mind.

As I headed back to the hut lodge, I refreshed with cold rainwater from a barrel kept outside. I could hear the sound of doves and monkeys howling from the mango tree. Auntie had heated water for lemongrass tea, sweetened it, and gave me a piece of flattened coconut bread she had tucked away in her bundles. Although I was already full from eating mangoes, I did not refuse her breakfast. "We are going Arabu to the field because I have work to do," she said.

Lucia Cayetano Guity

We walked uphill, leaving the seashore behind. The sun's rays were oppressive on a hot and humid day. When we arrived at the field, Auntie was on one side digging up root vegetables, yams, and yucca. I noticed she would cut the yucca plant branch into four pieces and replant it by just sticking it in the ground. I roamed around, handing her the sticks. As I stepped away from her, I noticed a snake with vibrant red, white, and black colors. As a six-year-old, I just admired it as it crawled away. This was my first experience seeing a snake, and I did not feel any fear.

Later, when we arrived back at the lodge, my Auntie explained to me that what we saw was a dangerous venomous snake that could cause death and told me never to chase after them. This memory sends shivers down my spine – the fear – a new discovery after hearing Aunt.

My experience with Auntie Wawa was an escapade that I will always cherish. The bond we shared was indelible. We headed back to the two-mile walk to the village the following morning after spending a weekend with my beloved Auntie Wawa.

Life between the ages of six and seven in Labuga was an exploration for a curious child like me. Our house perched high on the village hill offered a panoramic view. Two just minutes down the hill was the bay, which was bustling with activities most of the time. The other houses, scattered close by, most were Aunts and cousins mostly related. One Aunt had three Albino children: Omar, Gringa, and Arturo. Their grandfather, my uncle, was Albino as well, and they were part of my village. Ensured a lively atmosphere. Mornings began with the rooster's crow, followed by the murmur of neighbors' conversations. Privacy was scarce – if someone was sick, the whole village knew and would come to offer healing remedies or support.

The community extended well at the bottom of the hill, gushing with spring water and the bay. Women gathered there to bathe and collect water. Sometimes, they'd congregate near the bay, cleaning and salting fish and shrimp, which they then laid out to dry under the relentless sun. It was a customary process and a part of my early acculturation. Witnessing these strong-willed women butchering giant sharks with their grayish-smooth skin taught me the values of self-reliance and efficiency. My father's sister lived on that lower level of the hill. She was a very quiet woman but was filled with much knowledge and power in terms of land ownership.

My only childhood friend, Maryelena, and I would play around them, laughing and gossiping as girls do. We had a special bond forged over shared secrets and adventures. One memory we cherished was the majestic Papagallo tree by the bay. Its vibrant red flowers, resembling tiny roosters, would fall, and we'd eagerly collect them, savoring their sweet nectar.

While the women were busy, Maryelena and I would sneak into the cool embrace of the sea. Once, I got scratched by a submerged branch, a secret I confided only in her.

Our days were filled with religious instruction. Twice a week, Maryelena and I, assigned by our parents, would walk the narrow trails through tropical vegetation to the neighboring village of San Jose for Catechism classes. The matriarchal woman who taught us seemed kind and gentle. Learning our prayers was a fun experience for us. We graduated from these classes, marked by an afternoon treat at the Sacred Heart Parish Church. Gathered around a long mahogany table, all the children were welcomed by the priest who spoke about First Communion. Hot chocolate, tamales, and rolls awaited us - a truly memorable experience.

However, my memories of the actual First Communion ceremony are blurry. All I have is a picture of me on the altar, adorned in a beautiful white dress, a flower crown, and white gloves. This picture stands as my only childhood photograph.

Around this age, at six or seven, I was chosen to be a flower girl at the wedding of prominent villagers, Tina and Fafa. All I remember from the event is the searing pain inflicted by the hairdresser on my ears. It's funny how children tend to forget certain events, even significant ones. Nevertheless, I felt a sense of pride at being included in such celebrations.

It wasn't entertaining much, being the youngest amidst a house full of adults. While my older siblings gathered and conversed with neighbors, I'd roam the four-bedroom house. My favorite spot was my brother Julian's room, which had a window overlooking the scenic bay with palm trees and the Papagallo tree in the distance. He was away studying in Belize, a place I knew only through him. I'd rummage through his toolbox and play his records, leftover gifts from Uncle Tony, who ran an English school in Livingston. The records would repeat simple phrases:

"Chair. Silla. Table. Mesa. Bed. Cama."

No one knew I was there, listening intently to these records.

Another haven for me was my sister Simona's room. Rarely did I see her, for she studied in Guatemala City. Yet, I reveled in slathering Pond's cream on my face and arms, mimicking her by applying lipstick and powder. Her room, which was proof of her femininity, was decorated in pink with beautiful hats she learned to make at her economic apprenticeship school. Through their belongings, I felt a connection to these absent siblings.

My other four siblings and I shared a single room at night. Nightmares often led me to seek comfort beside my mother's bed.

The house's heart was the central living room, adorned with mahogany ornaments and furniture and kept meticulously tidy. An old-fashioned radio and a china cabinet added to its charm.

Christmas was a time of festive cheer. An artificial Christmas tree, seemingly to have been displayed for many years before my arrival, stood proudly. The miniature nativity scene with its angels, baby Jesus, lambs, and mules brought the story to life for me.

During these occasions, my elder sister, back from her studies, put her culinary skills to work in the kitchen. The aroma of spiced cakes with raisins, cookies, puddings, tamales, and "tuffies" (a local delicacy) filled the air. Hibiscus tea, also known as Jamaica flower drink, completed the festive spread. Food was plentiful, and I'd watch in fascination as the adults prepped, tasting, and licking spoons with a mischievous glint in my eye. Even the neighbors took part in the celebration. My mother, ever watchful, would swat my hand playfully, scolding me with a gentle smile, "Save some room for dinner, Mija!"

One Christmas, I recall the memory of being scared of the dark. As the celebration finally wound down sometime after midnight, exhausted from all the activity, everyone decided to attend the special Christmas Eve service at the church. Left alone, I drifted off to sleep on the living room couch.

Waking up in an empty house was terrifying. Pitch black surrounded me, the only sound the rustling of the night wind. Fearful of being truly alone, I stumbled outside. The familiar path down the hill to the bay, usually bustling with activity, was empty. Even the spot where the women cleaned fish was eerily quiet.

Streetlights offered a sliver of comfort on the way back up the hill. I found myself drawn to the familiar glow of the pharmacy at the corner, eventually settling on a cold sidewalk curb. A wave of relief washed over me when I saw my family returning. Dad scooped me up, my sleep-fogged mind barely registering anything until I was back in my bed.

Christmas morning brought a different kind of attention. Still chuckling about my nighttime adventure, my siblings teased me about being the only one to miss midnight mass.

The holiday spirit lingered well into January. Our village celebrated the New Year with a vibrant display of Garifuna culture. My father hired a group of *"Wanaragua"* dancers; their colorful costumes and energetic drumming attracted a crowd to our house.

Despite the festive atmosphere, the masks and the dancers' rapid movements terrified me. The rhythmic pounding of the drums and the constant clinking of shells on their ankles – like tiny rattlesnakes, I thought – only amplified my fear.

Thankfully, the festivities weren't all overwhelming. With Dad back home, we often took trips to the bay. He'd fish on one side of a small, rocky island with a lone palm tree while I splashed around in the crystal-clear water on the other. Afterward, I'd share stories of my adventures with Aunt Tia Wawa, and Dad would tell me about his life. This connection with him made me feel blessed to have him as my father.

One such afternoon, he pointed towards a cluster of twinkling lights in the distance. He said, "I am from over there. Do you see the little lights at a distance?"

I responded, "Yes, Dad."

"That's where your brother goes to school," he said, explaining it was across the sea in Belize. It was the first time I truly grasped the vastness of the world beyond our village.

My relationship with Dad was special. Mom always said I looked like him and even thought like him. Despite being the youngest, I felt a strong connection with him, a unique bond that transcended the usual sibling hierarchy.

One significant change was announced during one of these outings. Dad explained to me that I was going to move to Puerto Barrios along with Mom and my Brother because he was not returning to Belize to study, and instead, he and my brother Julian would be working for the American Fruit

Company. Weekends, however, would be spent back in Livingston.

As we left the island, the weight of the news settled in. The image of Dad carrying me back to shore after that conversation remains carved in my memory. We walked hand-in-hand up the familiar hill, a new chapter about to unfold in our lives.

The final memory of Labuga is blurry – a 4:00 am walk in the dark towards the ferry dock. The boat was crowded with people, some bundled in sweaters against the morning chill, others clutching luggage and purses. As the boat pulled away from the dock, I watched a group of pelicans on the pier disappear behind us. Suddenly, two playful dolphins appeared, swimming alongside the boat for a while before diving out of sight. Leaning against Mom for comfort, I drifted off to sleep, a faint smile playing on my lips. The warmth of her sweater and the gentle rocking of the ferry lulled me into a peaceful nap, a bittersweet farewell to the world I knew.

Chapter 3
Arrival At Puerto Barrios

When the boat finally arrived in Puerto Barrios, it was like stepping into a beehive. People were everywhere, yelling and calling out, even at six-thirty in the morning. The weather was hot and it was dusty outside. I saw horse-drawn carriages lined up on the side of the road and vendors selling food from carts. My father walked us to a small store run by an elderly man with a Jamaican accent named Don Andres. His shop was filled with colorful candies, cookies, and chilled sodas in an ice box. I had a grape Fanta and some cookies, and it tasted amazing. This was a much different welcome than I was used to in Labuga.

After the ferry ride, we took a long taxi ride through Puerto Barrios. We passed a train carrying what looked like loads of bananas. Finally, we arrived in a neighborhood past a hospital. Here, rows of gray duplex houses stood side-by-side. The view was something I had never seen before. These were the homes of the American Fruit Company employees, most of them Germans and Americans who worked at the port, shipping bananas all over the world. My father worked as a security guard there, and my brother Julian was also starting a new job.

The rows of gray duplex houses weren't just single units; they had separate kitchens in quarters one or two yards away from the main house. The first floor of our duplex housed the dining room. At the end of this room was my brother Julian's sleeping area, and two large bicycles stood parked to the side – the apparent mode of transportation during this era. Twelve stairs led up from outside to my father's bedroom, which he now shared with Mom. A large folding divider separated their sleeping area from the front corner that became my room. Attached to our duplex was another unit occupied by a couple with a boy around my age, 7. Sitting on the stairs, I gazed out at this new community and felt a sense of belonging for the first time since leaving Livingston. For the first time in my life, our whole family would be living together.

Most of my mornings were greeted by the lively calls of vendors calling out their wares: tamales, fresh milk, bread, and pastries. In the afternoons, they would come back selling toys, sweet treats, and my favorite baked Cookies quesadillas. My father would leave early for work and come home in the evening for dinner. There was a big fountain with running water next to our house, where the women would wash clothes and gossip. In the afternoons, when I had the place to myself, I loved taking showers in the cool, refreshing water.

Living in El Rastro was a whole new experience. Every evening before sunset, the entire neighborhood would gather in a field to fly kites. Kites of all shapes and sizes filled the sky, their bright colors a beautiful sight. It was like a competition whose was the largest, and we had our eyes on the blue skyline with kites flying with their splendor showcasing diverse colors of long wings and tails.

On Saturdays, we would take the ferry back to Livingston to visit my siblings, who were still there. We would bring them a treasure trove of food and treats from the American Fruit Company commissary, a supermarket only for employees. The commissary was a sensory overload in the best way possible. The aroma of fresh popcorn hung heavy in the air, competing with the sweet scent of strawberry ice cream. They even offered sliced salami and ham for you to taste! The aisles overflowed with exotic (to us) goods: colorful boxes of Corn Flakes cereal, bright red bottles of ketchup, steaming boxes of oatmeal, and a fridge section stocked with Coca-Cola cans. There was everything you could imagine, from fluffy white rice to an array of meats – a far cry from the limited selection in Livingston. We would pack our bags full of these goodies, eager to share them with our siblings back home. The ride back to Labuga Livingston was 40 minutes long in the afternoon, but it was always a delight. We'd watch dolphins leaping and playing in the waves and pelicans gliding effortlessly alongside the boat. It was a perfect end to a day filled with shopping and anticipation.

Back in Livingston, there would be a feast waiting for us, a joyous reunion filled with familiar faces. Everyone was eager to see us and devour the treats we brought from the American Fruit Company commissary. I wasted no time in joining my siblings in the kitchen. We bustled around, preparing the meal together. I'd eagerly dash out to our backyard, a fragrant haven overflowing with fresh herbs like basil, oregano, and thyme. Someone, usually an older sibling or a helpful neighbor, would assist with cutting and picking breadfruit from the gigantic tree that dominated our yard. The sound of laughter and conversation filled the air as elders, aunties, and villagers stopped by to visit. These evenings stretched late into the night, a testament to the strong sense of community. Some visitors would even stay over, bringing their hammocks or straw mats to lay down on our floor. Our home became a warm and welcoming haven for all who entered. After a week in Livingston, we would travel back to Puerto Barrios, where my father worked.

Then, in 1962, something scary happened. Cuba dropped a bomb right near our neighborhood in Puerto Barrios! I saw green airplanes and a big orange explosion in the sky. We all had to hide under beds and tables to protect ourselves. The next day, we moved to the house of my father's friend in Puerto Barrios City. His daughter, Vilma, became my best friend, and I also had another friend named Lucy, who was beautiful with blonde hair and green eyes. We were like the three musketeers!

We lived in my father's friend's house for a while, and then we moved a few more times. My brother Julian eventually went to the United States to join the military. Finally, my father retired from the American Fruit Company and bought land in Puerto Barrios. There, he built a beautiful house and opened a store called Tienda La Florida. I pretty much lived off the candy from the store, taking it to school to share with my friends. My brother Julian would send me records by the Beatles and other rock and roll bands like the Rolling Stones, and we would play them during recess at school, dancing under a tree. I became a fan.

One day, I noticed a little boy around the house. I had no idea my mother had been pregnant! No one had explained it to me. This new brother, Freddie, was four years old when I was nine, and I could recall him calling me baby sister, which annoyed me. It seemed like grown-ups never explained things to kids back then. They would just move you somewhere new or introduce a new person into your life without any warning. Now, our family has grown to eight!

My brother Julian kept in touch with us by mail and would send us packages. One time, he sent a Statue of Liberty made of silver metal. It sat in the living room, and I would often admire it, not knowing what it meant. I finally asked my father, and he told me that Santa Claus lived there, in the North. My imagination ran wild!

School in Puerto Barrios was a pleasant experience. Every day, I walked a mile to school with a group of neighborhood kids. We crossed a bridge, enjoying the warm, sunny climate of our new home. We'd grab guavas and almonds from trees lining the unpaved streets. School started with a delicious treat: hot, sweetened milk with sweet buns. There was one thing I disliked, though – a monthly dose of some kind of orange, syrupy dewormer, or gluey medicine.

The teachers were great role models – mature, poised, and always dressed sharply. We, the students, wore striped blue and white plaid skirts and white blouses. My academics were good, and I enjoyed school with my best friends, Vilma and Lucy. Vilma was my loud and protective friend, while Lucy was the model of the group, and I was the most reserved shy one among us. We were the three musketeers!

On Guatemala's Independence Day, September 15th, all the students participated in a parade. We were lined up by height, with the tallest students leading the way and the shortest bringing up the rear. Being tall, I marched proudly in the front row with my two musketeers right behind the flag carrier. It was an exciting experience and my last time marching through the streets of Puerto Barrios.

Soon after, my father sold our house with the store and built a smaller one closer to school, about a half-mile away. The new house was painted gray with green window frames, offering a beautiful view and close access to the Amatique Bay. We could even see large ships sailing towards Matias de Galves Port. This new location also meant easy access to the beach. One afternoon, I witnessed a thrilling sight – a visible shark fin heading towards the port! These were quiet moments I'd cherish forever.

One day, my father even went fishing. He had a large canoe vessel powered by a Johnson motor. He returned home with a giant, six-foot fish with a big head! Our fridge wasn't big enough to hold it, so my father sent me and one of my older sisters to sell the fish at the market. Someone with a cartwheel helped us carry the massive creature, and it was sold out within thirty minutes! At just ten years old, I had my first taste of entrepreneurship.

This new house also had a river running behind it, an almond tree in one corner, and a miniature coconut tree in the front that produced large, easily reachable coconuts. My mom planted a small garden with oregano and a leafy green vegetable called chipilin. We even had pets – a puppy named Diana, two rabbits, and a medium-sized turtle that would disappear into the river for a month, only to return bigger!

Lucia Cayetano Guity

The neighborhood was a vibrant mix of ethnicities. There were Ladinos (mixed Spanish and indigenous), redheaded Spaniards, and Black Creoles of Jamaican descent. It was a stark contrast to our Garifuna village in Livingston, where everyone was Garifuna. Here, we were known as the family with many homes.

The Statue of Liberty continues to hold a special place in my heart. I'd often admire it, filled with curiosity about the place it represented.

One day, everything changed. My father and older sisters disappeared without any explanation. My little brother, now four years old, and my sister, Jovita, were left with my mom. We didn't discuss their absence; we just learned to adapt.

One time, my mom sent Jovita and me to visit Don Andres, the old man with the shop near the port, the one I met when I first arrived in Puerto Barrios. He was much older now but still kind. He gave us candies and cookies, and we learned that my father had gone "north," where Santa Claus lived, according to him. We said goodbye to Don Andres and headed to the train tracks near the pier. There, we saw mountains of yellow bananas on the ground, and everyone was helping themselves. It seemed like the end of an era with the Fruit Company.

My mom was happy with the bananas, and the next day, she made banana bread and sent me to sell it from house to house. I followed her instructions and sold all the bread. One man even offered me five dollars for a single loaf, but I refused and kept it for myself to eat. That was my last time selling banana bread. One day, Mom called me to her room and braided my hair, also massaging my neck since I suffered from thyroid, according to her. I never had any problems as far as I knew.

Soon after, a stern-looking Garifuna woman named Diana moved in as our nanny. My mom seemed to disappear, and this woman dictated our every move, not allowing me to go anywhere. My sister Jovita mostly stayed at her friend's house. It was a lonely time, and I felt the separation from my parents more than ever. The Statue of Liberty became my idol, a symbol of the North where my father was and where Santa Claus lived, according to what I'd been told.

Around this time, I remember hearing something about a man walking on the moon on the radio. There was a joyous commotion in the background, and it sparked a new curiosity in me. This news, along with my family's strange situation, made me realize there was a whole world beyond Labuga Livingston and Puerto Barrios, and my family was now scattered somewhere unknown.

One day, I found myself on a bus ride with my two siblings to Guatemala City. We were going to live with a registered nurse named Dona Rita, her husband, and their two grown

daughters, who looked like models, beautiful young ladies. I
don't remember the seven-hour journey; it was like a blur.
Suddenly, I was in a bustling city, a stark contrast to the quiet
life I knew in Puerto Barrios. Buses and cars honked their
horns, creating a constant symphony of sound.

Dona Rita's house had a large gate and a concrete wall that
functioned as a storefront. Inside, a small corridor opened into
a courtyard with a garden, a laundry area, a shower room, and
a bathroom. Three bedrooms surrounded this central space.
Ours was near the front, followed by a large living room with a
sitting area then the kitchen and dining area. After dinner, we
all gathered in the living room to watch television for the first
time. I was mesmerized by musicals and Spanish comedies, a
welcome distraction from my worries.

Dona Rita and her family were kind and treated us well
despite some tension with one of the daughters, who seemed
upset when someone used her towel. After that, I was careful
not to upset her with anything.

On Sundays, we were treated to movies, walks to the park,
and window shopping. During our stay, a lawyer would pick us
up and take us to get our passports. I remember having my
photo taken, a glimpse of a future life in America. We were
also informed that we were minors and needed an adult to
travel with us. Thankfully, our green cards were approved.

Months passed before my oldest sister, Simona, arrived from New York to reunite us with our parents. She took us to a hotel and provided us with new outfits. I remember a yellow dress with a white collar, black boots, and a long black wig that made me giggle. We enjoyed a breakfast of delicious bread, pastries, refried beans, eggs, and milk.

I am grateful to Dona Rita for taking us in. Though we weren't a perfect family unit, there was a sense of love and support in her home. Dona Rita was a friend to my older sister Chiqui, and her connections proved invaluable during this time. I also appreciate the sacrifices my parents made to bring all their children to the United States in the most honorable way. I'm thankful to the lawyer and the nanny from Puerto Barrios who likely made that seven-hour-long bus ride to Guatemala City with us young children. Even though I don't remember the ride itself, it's a testament to the lengths people go to for family. Perhaps it's how a child's mind works, selectively holding onto memories.

The long-awaited day finally arrived. At eleven years old in 1967, I, along with my oldest sister Simona, my youngest brother Freddie (seven years old), and Jovita (fourteen years old), boarded a Pan American Airlines first-class flight from Aurora Airport in Guatemala City. The service was incredible. I vividly remember the delicious hot meal with steak and a variety of desserts. It was a far cry from the simple life I had known in Livingston and a taste of the new life that awaited us in the United States.

Chapter 4

The Great Migration

The airplane dipped below the clouds, and I was completely taken away by the sight of a million twinkling fireflies, no, a million tiny diamonds scattered across a vast, inky canvas – that's what New York City looked like at night. Mesmerized, I pressed my face against the window, a million questions swirling in my head about this new journey that I was about to start.

We landed with a thud that jolted me back to reality. Sounds were everywhere – the loud engines, people talking excitedly, and quick announcements coming from the loudspeaker. Following my sister's lead, I disembarked, feeling a knot of nervousness tighten in my stomach. Would I ever feel comfortable in this bustling metropolis?

Emerging from the airport, landmarks like the Statue of Liberty and the Empire State Building were pointed out by my sister, each sight adding to the surreal experience of our first night in America.

We landed smoothly, and although the details of the ride from the airport are hazy, I vividly remember arriving in the Bronx, where my new home on Trinity Avenue Street awaited. The apartment building settled on the third floor felt like a maze with its narrow hallway leading to a small kitchen on the right, followed by a bathroom, and then opening into a living room. It was here that I reunited with most of my siblings, except for my brother, Julian, who was serving in the Military in Vietnam, and my sister, Chiqui, who was in Florida. Sister Chiqui was always somewhere else, and I barely remember what she looked like in person because she was rarely home. From what I understand, she moved to Florida to live with a Garifuna relative. After falling ill, she had to return to Guatemala City for surgery, and that's where she met Dona Rita, the head nurse who played a significant role in our lives. Dona Rita generously sponsored our stay in Guatemala City, helping us tremendously during a challenging time. Chiqui's life took another turn when she met someone from Belize and started living with him. Anyway, I missed her when we arrived in New York.

My father's embrace was warm and welcoming, a comforting assurance after the long journey. The apartment was overcrowded, with only one bedroom for all of us to share, but the joy of being reunited with my family overshadowed any discomfort. This arrangement, however, wasn't ideal for everyone. My sister Vila had a son who required adequate housing, an environment less confined than our one-bedroom apartment could offer. We were together again, although in a tight space, but it was our space.

The following days were a whirlwind of activity. I learned that my father had left Guatemala and landed in New Orleans. He told me stories about how he went to a restaurant, and Black Americans were outside peeping through the window, concerned that he would not be served. Thankfully, the restaurant's white owners surprised him. Not only was he warmly welcomed, but he initiated a conversation with them about the American Fruit Company, his former employer. They were familiar with the company, and the conversation flowed easily. The meal ended with him sipping on a glass of cognac, a luxurious treat amidst the unexpected turn of events.

However, the city was facing a different kind of unrest. Civil tensions crackled in the air, a stark contrast to the peaceful life he had left behind in Guatemala. Despite the initial warmth of the restaurant owners, New Orleans wasn't a place he felt his family could build a secure future.

Then came a stroke of luck. The same restaurant owner, impressed by my father's demeanor and perhaps recognizing his potential, offered him a lifeline. He recommended my father for a job at a custom jewelry company in New York City. It was a chance to escape the tensions and pursue a career in a field he knew well. This unexpected opportunity presented a difficult choice: relocate his life yet again, leaving the familiar behind for the unknown. My mother, ever resourceful, secured a job with a Jewish family on Long Island. Through their sponsorship, she was able to obtain a green card, a crucial step in our journey to becoming American citizens. She then sponsored my father, and together they sponsored all of us, their children. It was a long and arduous process, but their sacrifices were paving the way for a better future for all of us.

Our living situation improved when my father managed to find a larger apartment on the same street, Trinity Avenue. This one had two spacious bedrooms and a large living room. Even better, it was on the fourth floor, a walk-up, but that meant a bit of exercise after all the delicious food my mother was preparing. The building was filled with familiar faces – Garifuna friends of my father's who had worked with him at the American Fruit Company back in Guatemala. Weekends were filled with laughter and music as we visited each other's homes, sharing stories and enjoying a taste of our homeland in this new city. My older Sister Simona would throw parties at her apartment, a block from us. She would cook and sell beer and sodas, and that is how the years progressed into the seventies.

My school, Junior High School 120, was just a block away from our apartment. This proximity was a blessing; I didn't have to navigate the complexities of the subway system yet.

My mother, ever resourceful, continued to work for the Ross family in Long Island five days a week. Mrs. Ross, a kind and generous woman, treated us like family. During the summers, she'd pick us up – me, my father, and Mom – to spend time with her and her family at their charming cottage on Fire Island. The entire family and guests would pitch in, grilling food and setting up the outdoor space.

Mark, Mrs. Ross's son who was a year older than me, was an adventurous soul. He'd lead me on sailing expeditions on his veiled boat, and together, we'd dig for clams in the shallows, unearthing hidden treasures beneath the sand. As evening approached, we'd walk to the other side of the island, chasing the setting sun and building elaborate sandcastles that mimicked the grandeur of the city skyline we'd soon return to.

Back at the cottage, I'd play fetch with their dog, a furry companion who welcomed me with boundless enthusiasm. The Ross family showered us with delicious meals – burgers, hot dogs, and fluffy donuts. Mrs. Ross, with a touch of extravagance, would pack me beautiful clothes as gifts. These weren't your average finds – designer brands from Saks Fifth Avenue adorned with tags that read "Gucci" and "Prada." They were a world away from my usual hand-me-downs, and while some kids at school mocked me for them by questioning me why I wore designer labels, I knew the story behind these clothes. They were a symbol of Mrs. Ross's generosity and a glimpse into a different world, a world of luxury and privilege.

Mrs. Ross, a woman with a passion for learning, wouldn't let the weekend be solely about fun and games. Before leaving, she'd hand me a stack of magazines she and her college-aged daughter no longer needed. Vogue, Time, and other publications, along with the hefty New York Times Sunday edition, filled my arms. I spent hours poring over these magazines, marveling at the Rolex watches gleaming on perfectly manicured wrists and models showcasing the latest fashion trends. The New York Times, with its in-depth articles on current events, opened a window to a world beyond the confines of the Bronx. This exposure to different ways of life and the vastness of knowledge seemed to have helped me adapt to a different life in the States.

My immersion in American life wasn't confined to the Ross family's generosity and the world glimpsed through magazines. I also accompanied my older sisters to night school, where I'd sit quietly, learning lessons. This exposure not only reinforced my rapid learning of English but also fueled my desire to be a part of a more advanced class.

However, the bilingual class I was placed in initially felt like a roadblock to my progress. It was filled with Spanish-speaking students, and I worried it would slow down my learning. With the help of an interpreter, I gathered the courage to speak with the school principal. I explained my desire to immerse myself in English and requested a transfer to a more challenging class.

The principal, impressed by my initiative, arranged for a placement exam the following day. With all that determination, I successfully scored 98% on that exam. This score earned me a spot in a class with the "elite and popular students," as they were called.

While this move placed me amongst the top students, it also attracted some unwanted attention. A girl named Liza, perhaps feeling threatened by my sudden arrival, sent a threatening note, promising to "jump me" in gym class. Instead of backing away, I decided to confront her head-on. During lunch break, I approached her group, ignoring the butterflies fluttering in my stomach. With a calmness that surprised even me, I informed her about my "dental appointment" that conveniently clashed with gym class. The unexpectedness of my response disarmed her. Her initial smirk transformed into a flustered mumble as her friends burst out laughing. This encounter, though brief, proved to be a turning point. Liza never bothered me again, and her friends, initially wary, began approaching me with curiosity. I became friends with her but never let her get close. This experience taught me a valuable lesson about navigating social dynamics, a skill that would serve me well in the future.

I seemed to have to adjust and adapt to my new environment real quick. I had to relate to student peers from different cultures and countries. I had Puerto Rican friends,

Cubans, Dominicans, students from South Carolina, and African Americans. The teachers were extremely endearing and supportive. One would often compliment me on my smile, a simple gesture that boosted my confidence. My dedicated counselor saw potential. She nominated me for a program called "Keuka College Summer Experience," a three-week program offering academic classes in the mornings and social activities in the afternoons. This opportunity, a chance to experience college life firsthand, filled me with excitement, but the thought of being away from my family for three weeks was daunting.

With my counselor's encouragement and my parents' blessing, I embarked on this new adventure. Keuka College, situated amidst rolling hills, was far from the bustling streets of the Bronx. My dorm room was simple but comfortable, and my roommates, girls from different parts of New York State, were friendly and welcoming.

The classes were challenging but stimulating. Mornings were spent grappling with complex math problems and diving deep into the world of English literature. The afternoons offered a welcome break, filled with activities like swimming in the lake, rowing on a quaint wooden boat, and even a thrilling trip to an amusement park. In the evenings, we gathered for lively discussions, movie nights, and unprepared dance parties. It was an incredible experience, a gateway to the freedom and independence that college life offered.

One night, at a dance party, I met an African-American boy. He was a year older than me with cute green eyes. We spent the evening talking about everything and nothing, our laughter mingling with the music. As the night drew to a close, he walked me back to my dorm room. Under the soft glow of the streetlamp, he leaned in and gave me my first kiss. It was a sweet, innocent gesture that sent butterflies fluttering in my stomach.

Another weekend was arranged to visit Niagara Falls. I enjoyed the thundering roar of the water and the breathtaking mist that wrapped everything in its path. It was a truly awe-inspiring experience.

The last week, I took an exam on English literature, where I had to write an essay on my experience at Keuka College and what I learned there. My math skills also improved – I scored 89%! Not bad at all.

I was incredibly grateful that my school counselor saw potential in me. She nominated me for this amazing program, and I wouldn't have had this opportunity without her belief in me. I also didn't see any of the students from my school throughout the program – we were selected from various schools across New York State.

My thanks also go to my father for trusting his daughter to be away from home for three weeks. It meant a lot to me. And to my sister Vila, who sent a thoughtful package with goodies and some money (even though it got removed by security!). The feeling was what mattered most. The program provided us with spending money as well, and that was sufficient.

The day came when we were loaded onto the buses. There were several buses with different destinations. As I boarded, I saw the green-eyed boy who gave me my first kiss. I took a moment to thank him for the experience. We waved goodbye to each other, his bus heading towards a different destination than mine. All the way back home, I cherished every minute of this experience – one that is imprinted in my mind forever.

In September, I would start at a newly constructed high school named Herbert H. Lehman High School. It was located on the other side of town, and I'd need to take the bus, which required a monthly fare. The school was brand new and boasted a more diverse population than my previous one. I even heard there were protests from the community against the plan to bus inner-city students like myself to a predominantly Greek, Italian, and Irish neighborhood. Thankfully, these protests weren't successful.

As a newcomer to the States, addressing from the Caribbean coast, I was still learning to navigate the nuances of people's expressions. Yet, I came with a strong sense of self, my own values, principles, and morals. Above all, I loved my parents dearly and wanted to do my best to express my gratitude for their sacrifices. So, with that in mind, I was ready to head into this new school, focused on learning and everything it had to offer.

Chapter 5
Life In USA

Moving to New York City was a big change for me. Adjusting to life in New York was a journey filled with both challenges and discoveries. After the initial overwhelming reunion with my family, I had to navigate the complexities of life in a bustling city that was very different from anywhere I'd lived before.

The streets of the Bronx were noisy and often dirty, a far cry from the serene, natural beauty of Livingston. I was struck by small cultural differences, such as people eating on the go, a sight that contrasted sharply with the disciplined meal times back home that my mom taught us. I can recall a day when I saw a man eating something with cheese dripping on his hands; that's when I learned about Pizza.

My early days were marked by the struggle to overcome language barriers. I remember feeling helpless when a woman at the supermarket seemed frustrated with me for not holding the door, a simple act of courtesy that I didn't understand at the time due to the language gap. These small misunderstandings were learning moments that gradually helped me adapt to the local customs and behaviors.

Our first apartment on Trinity Avenue was noisy and crowded, but it was our first home in America. It wasn't the safest place, though, and something scary happened to me in my sister's building. One day, I was visiting my older sister's building one block from my parents. When I reached her building, I walked up the stairs and realized that someone was trying to assault me by throwing me underneath the stairs. I fought and ran, dashing out of the building. That's when Dad knew we needed to find a better place to live.

During this period, two of my sisters got married. The one with the child managed to take her son out of the children's home and moved out to live with her husband. The other sister married and left with her husband to live together.

Recognizing the need for a better quality of life, especially with some of my siblings starting their own families, my father, with help from my brother Julian, who had recently returned from military service, secured a better apartment in a more pleasant community. This new home was close to both the Bronx Zoo and the New York Botanical Garden, areas that provided a much-needed escape from the urban grind. The new apartment was part of a development that offered not only safety but also a sense of community that had been lacking on Trinity Avenue.

I left Trinity Avenue, which was plagued with the Ford Apache Gangs and was unsafe. The new community offered an easy commute by bus to my new school, Herbert H. Lehman High School, which was also brand new. One could smell its freshness and admire its modern structure built over the Hitchington River Parkway. The building was iconic. I felt blessed, sensing that God was divinely guiding my path. I was thrilled to have my brother Julian residing on the third floor of our complex, and one of my married sisters moved to the fourth floor of the same complex. My parents, two other siblings, and I occupied a three-bedroom apartment on the second floor.

Living here was like being in a utopia. Just a block away on Crotona Avenue lay a vibrant Little Italy, renowned for its fresh produce and seafood, and markets stocked with items imported from Italy, such as Parmigiano Reggiano, olive oils, prosciutto, and sausages that hung from the ceiling, filling the air with their pungent aromas. The famous Arthur Avenue was just around the corner. I particularly enjoyed the Gelateria, where they made gelato that became a delightful weekend treat. The local pizzeria offered thin, crunchy pizzas that were a favorite. Every Sunday after church, my mom and I would stroll down these streets, soaking in the sights, sounds, and aromas—whether the sweet smell from the bakeries, the warm scent of fresh bread, or the sharper smells of dried sausages and mozzarella. These walks became a cherished ritual, as did visits to the Bronx Zoo and Botanical Garden, where the children played happily with their cousins.

Even though we were happy in our new home, we still missed Guatemala sometimes. It was sad when my grandma passed away back there. It made us remember our family there.

Life in New York kept changing. New music and dances became popular, like disco. It was a fun time! We celebrated together, throwing parties filled with laughter and music. Weekends were for exploring the city as a family. We picnicked in the vast expanse of Central Park, the emerald heart of New York City. Winter brought the magical transformation of the park's ice rink, where I have vivid memories of falling on the ice, followed by the warmth of hot cocoa and crispy French fries smothered in ketchup. These simple moments, filled with family and joy, became etched in my memory forever.

Similar to my childhood in Labuga Livingston, shopping trips to Macy's became a cherished tradition. Especially after the Thanksgiving Day parade, the energy in the store was electric. Life seemed to be moving at a whirlwind pace, a constant swirl of new experiences and discoveries. The era of disco throbbed with a contagious energy, while the news was dominated by the shocking death of Elvis Presley and the unfolding Watergate scandal. It felt like I was on a thrilling roller coaster ride, a whirlwind of joy and learning.

Speaking of learning that seemed to be very struggling yet thriving, next up is my high school experience – a whole new chapter waiting to be explored!

Chapter 6

Learning Across Borders

Education was a precious commodity in my Garifuna family. Its roots are traced back to my indomitable grandmother, Lasara Sandoval Gonzales. Exiled from St. Vincent to Honduras and eventually settling in Labuga Livingston, Guatemala, she faced hardship head-on. A single mother of five children, Lasara built a life of self-reliance. She acquired land, nurtured it, and planted fruit trees that nourished generations. Another one of her properties was used to grow rice. After my grandmother passed, one of my sisters built a house on the property, and during the excavation of the fire there were tons of yams of different varieties. The green vegetation that covered the ground had developed much edible yam throughout the years cultivated by grandma. Even today, the land bears witness to her legacy. A majestic avocado tree, planted years before I was born, continues to provide fruit, its long, pear-shaped bounty a testament to her labor of love.

My mother's education was cut short in the second grade. Lasara needed her help on the farm, a place the Garifuna called "arabu." Despite this, my mother never forgot the importance of learning. The Bible became our primary source of education, and I vividly remember reciting poems and homework while standing on a table – a testament to her dedication.

My formal education began in Guatemala, where I had the privilege of attending kindergarten. I firmly believe that early childhood education is crucial for a child's development, laying the foundation for cognitive skills and social interaction outside the family unit.

Guatemala also gifted me with Spanish, my third language. Being fluent in Spanish has proven invaluable throughout my life, both in my career and travels. I can now communicate and translate between Spanish, English, and Garifuna, even dabbling in Italian, French, and Arabic!

In 1967, at the age of nine, my life took an unexpected turn. My family immigrated to New York City, a decision made by my father to secure a better future for his children. While I wasn't part of the discussion, I trusted his plan.

The cultural shift was immense, but I adapted. School, however, presented a new challenge. Placed in a Spanish-speaking class, I felt my English wasn't progressing. So, at just fifteen years old, I took charge of my education. I advocated for myself, speaking to the principal and requesting a class designed for English learners. They tested me, and my determination earned me a spot in a more challenging program. This experience was a turning point, teaching me the importance of speaking up for my needs.

My hard work paid off. Graduating from junior high, I even received the honor of attending a prestigious three-week summer program at Keuka College. It was an eye-opening experience, showcasing the vast possibilities that awaited me.

Back in New York City, I embarked on a new chapter at Herbert H. Lehman High School. The school, with its modern architecture and classrooms hovering over a highway, felt symbolic – a new path built upon past experiences. The teachers were dedicated and encouraging. A familiar face from my elementary school even offered a comforting smile, reminding me that even in a new environment, there could be familiarity. Some teachers, like Mr. McDermott, embodied the spirit of the hippie era with their earthy demeanor. I, too, embraced self-expression through patched jeans and embroidered tops, a look that became my signature.

Academics were a thrilling journey. I continued to hone my Spanish skills, but this time by choice. English, math, science, and even investment classes filled my schedule. The investment class took us on a field trip to Wall Street, where we witnessed the bustling heart of the stock market in action. My nursing class visited the Bronx Lebanon Hospital, where I later volunteered as a candy striper. While feeding patients and learning proper bed-making techniques were rewarding experiences, the visit to the morgue was a bit unsettling!

Lucia Cayetano Guity

High school wasn't just about textbooks. I actively participated in extracurricular activities. Relay races on the track and field team tested my teamwork skills. The leadership club allowed me to plan events and even try gymnastics, a fun way to challenge myself physically. But it was the outdoors club that truly ignited my adventurous spirit. We explored Appalachian mountain trails, camped under starry skies, and rode horses at dude ranches. These experiences not only fostered survival skills but also provided opportunities to connect with a diverse group of classmates - Irish, Italian, Greek, African American, and, of course, Garifuna. It was a beautiful tapestry of cultures and experiences woven together with laughter and joy.

After four years of high school, I felt a deep sense of accomplishment. Living in the States has not only strengthened me but also broadened my horizons. I learned about American history and the rich tapestry of cultures woven into its fabric. While I embraced my Garifuna heritage, I never lost myself in the mix. Respecting individuality was a crucial lesson for a developing mind.

At seventeen, on the cusp of eighteen, I was a tall and skinny young woman, often mistaken for a model. My height sometimes made me feel out of place, longing to be shorter. Despite volunteering as a candy striper, I encountered some unwelcome attention, which I learned to navigate firmly.

Seeking a more structured environment, I joined a work-study program, becoming an X-ray technician in Dr. Berkowitz's office. Learning to operate the X-ray machine and develop film was a valuable experience. During summers, I earned extra money maintaining parks with a youth program, fostering teamwork and a sense of community responsibility.

These experiences instilled a sense of financial independence. I opened my first bank account with a mere twenty dollars and gradually grew it through various means. Helping my older sister with childcare and food prep for her catering business taught me valuable cooking skills.

June 1975 marked a significant milestone – my high school graduation. With honors and a Regents' Excellence award in foreign languages, I stood tall despite attending the ceremony alone. My family, bound by work commitments, couldn't be there. This experience underscored my growing maturity and independence.

That fall, I enrolled at Bronx Community College. However, self-doubt gnawed at me. Having arrived in the US seven years prior with limited English proficiency, the thought of college felt daunting. But I pushed past these fears, enrolling in the entrance exam. While I excelled, the requirement for an English as a Second Language (ESL) class felt like a setback.

Lucia Cayetano Guity

The Bronx Community College campus was a beautiful sight, nestled amidst lush greenery and historical monuments. Navigating registration was a challenge, but I tackled it with determination. Algebra and trigonometry initially proved difficult, but with the help of two wonderful tutors – a Jewish woman who mentored me and an African American man who guided me through philosophy – I conquered these obstacles. My professors and tutors became more than educators; they became acquaintances who broadened my world. A music teacher even invited me to a party in Manhattan, where I met prominent figures in the art and music industry.

Though Bronx Community College was known for its nursing program, my interests shifted. Excelling in sociology, particularly the exploration of cultures and ethnicities, I wrote a captivating essay on this very topic. Immersing myself in the nuances of human behavior based on culture and experiences became a deep passion.

In 1978, I graduated from Bronx Community College with merit and a coveted spot on the Dean's List VIP for academic excellence. This recognition was a huge confidence booster, proving my efforts were paying off.

While friendships were scarce, with most students focused on work and family, my parents and sister celebrated my graduation at a joyous dinner.

My journey continued at Herbert H. Lehman College, a four-year institution. However, thanks to my 69 transferable credits from Bronx Community College, I only needed to attend for two years.

Imagine my surprise when my African American tutor from Bronx Community College became my sociology professor at Lehman! The world seemed smaller. My growing passion for culture and ethnicity led me to join the Social Work Department. Here, I met wonderful students who shared similar interests. Janice, in particular, became a close friend and confidante. Between classes and during lunch breaks, we spent countless hours engaged in stimulating conversations.

My social work curriculum focused on social sciences and liberal arts. Field placements at establishments like Morningside Nursing Home provided valuable hands-on experience. Working with groups and families caring for the elderly, I specialized in gerontology. Collaboration with other healthcare professionals – nurses, physical therapists, pastoral care providers – was an essential part of the team approach to patient care.

Balancing school and work demanded a rigorous schedule. Three days a week were dedicated to my social work internship, and two days to my studies. This whirlwind experience was a crucible, shaping me into a professional.

There was no time to spare, but my resolve to succeed only grew stronger. Shyness gave way to confidence as I tackled challenges, honed my problem-solving skills, and learned to delegate tasks. Developing empathy and compassion became central to my approach, empowering individuals and families to navigate their situations.

One day, a flyer on a school bulletin board advertising a caregiving position for an elderly woman caught my eye. Eager for additional income and a change from the endless pizza diet my student budget afforded, I decided to apply. This undergraduate internship wasn't paid, and looking professional was paramount. My father, struggling to fully support my education, had delivered an ultimatum: choose school or work. Determined to do both, I called the woman on the flyer.

She lived in a luxurious apartment on Manhattan's prestigious 68th Street and Fifth Avenue. A uniformed butler ushered me in, where I met the woman and discussed my duties. Accompanying her to the Metropolitan Museum of Art was part of the job description – a perk that appealed to my artistic side, fostered in my music and art classes at Bronx Community College.

Pushing her wheelchair through the museum's vast halls, we engaged in stimulating conversations about art. Lunch at the museum's restaurant was a delightful experience. Her choice of French onion soup – my first encounter with this savory combination of broth, bread, and melted cheese – was a revelation. The conversation flowed easily, covering current events and a range of topics that revealed her sharp wit and zest for life.

Returning to her apartment, she surprised me with a generous payment of $150. This weekly Saturday job became a lifesaver, helping me cover college expenses until graduation in 1981.

My graduation ceremony was a proud moment. My parents and sister, beaming with joy, witnessed me receive my Bachelor's Degree in Social Work. My professor, recognizing my potential, recommended me for a position with the Dominican Sisters of the Sick and Poor, a family home health service organization.

Working as part of a team of healthcare professionals, I provided services to individuals and families in the community. Visiting nurses, home health aides, pastoral care providers, and social workers like myself formed a vital support network. These community visits were often challenging. Sometimes, I encountered unsafe living conditions that necessitated finding alternative housing for the patients, ensuring a safe environment for both patients and healthcare providers. Dressed in our professional navy blue suits and white shirts, we became a familiar and trusted presence in the community.

After a year of dedicated service, I craved a change. Thirteen years had passed since I left Guatemala, and a yearning for my homeland filled me. Now a confident 24-year-old American citizen, I felt a transformation within. With a renewed sense of independence, I booked a plane ticket, eager to reconnect with my roots.

At the airport, a chance encounter with a Garifuna woman embarking on the same journey sparked a new connection. Little did I know this meeting would pave the way for the next chapter in my life's journey...

Chapter 7

Homecoming

In July 1981, I returned to Guatemala as a young adult, eager to reconnect with my roots. The journey started with a Greyhound bus ride to Puerto Barrios, which took six hours. Seated next to me was a Garifuna woman who talked incessantly about her son. She spoke of him with such pride and devotion that I imagined he was a young boy, although I never asked his age. The journey was filled with vibrant scenery, and each rest stop was bustling with vendors selling tortillas with boiled eggs and salt, refreshments in small plastic bags, and slices of mango, peanuts, and cashew nuts. I abstained from buying anything, nibbling on my own snacks and sipping on mineral water I had bought in Guatemala City.

Upon arriving in Puerto Barrios, the intense heat greeted us—typical for this port, where temperatures soared to 110 degrees. The woman and I shared a taxi to the port's dock to board a ferry boat to Livingston. As we sailed away, the cool breeze was refreshing, and the ride evoked memories of my first ferry journey with Mom and Dad when we left Livingston.

When we arrived in Livingston, I felt a mix of nostalgia and excitement. The dock was crowded, and an elderly man with a cart offered to carry my suitcase. I asked him to take me to my godmother's house in San Jose village. Along the way, I noticed that my old house in Barrio Barrique had been looted and was now inhabited by others. As we walked through the central avenue, a young man working on a construction site greeted me warmly, asking how long I would be in town. I responded that I would stay for about a week.

My primary school teacher still lived in her yellow house on the corner street. She was now retired but welcomed me with her usual gentle smile when I stopped by her store to greet her. Finally, we reached my godmother Saa's house, where she embraced me with a nurturing smile. Her husband and niece, Gisela, were also there. Gisela and I, being the same age, planned to visit a disco lounge by the bay that night. Despite my godmother's overprotective concerns, we went and danced the night away, enjoying the cool sea breeze.

The next day, we organized a picnic at Queweche River, a thirty-five-minute walk from town along the seashore. Our group of ten, including the woman from the bus and her son— the same young man I had seen working on the house— brought along food and drinks. We had a fantastic time, took lots of pictures, and swam in the river. However, a sharp sea shell cut my toe, causing it to bleed. The woman's son quickly rinsed my toe and applied a bandage, ending our picnic early. Despite the injury, we went back to the disco lounge that night and danced until dawn, my throbbing toe forgotten in the joy of the moment.

Leaving Guatemala was bittersweet. I cherished the time spent with my elderly aunts, Tia WaWa and Tia Caya, and my godmother. Upon returning to the States, my father was upset that our house in Livingston was not available for my use. He decided we would rebuild it with concrete, ensuring his children would never be homeless.

Two years later, at a dance party hosted by my brother Julian, who worked as a DJ, I encountered the young man who had treated my toe in Livingston. We danced and exchanged numbers, and six months later, he asked my father for my hand in marriage. On June 23rd, 1984, I got married to Edward Edgar Guity at St. Martin of Tours Church. My father proudly walked me down the aisle, and the ceremony was officiated by Father Plow, who prayed over us for an hour. It was a joyous occasion, attended by friends, family, and colleagues. Dancing with my father was one of the highlights of the day.

After our honeymoon, my parents retired to Guatemala. Tragically, my father passed away from cardiac complications shortly after. The news shattered my world. My sister Chiqui and I immediately arranged for flights to Guatemala City. Upon arriving in Livingston, I collapsed from grief, realizing the deep bond I had with my father.

To cope with the loss, I enrolled at Fordham University School of Social Work. I left my job at Dominican Sisters Family Health Services and began working at Bedford Hills Correctional Facility, the only maximum-security prison for women in New York State. Fordham did not allow me to complete my internship at Dominican Sisters, but Bedford

Hills granted me employment as a counselor and allowed me to practice my internship in their Family Violence Program.

I spent six years working at Bedford Hills, where I developed counseling groups and provided individual therapy to inmates. Many of the women were mothers, spouses, or daughters who faced significant challenges. As a bilingual counselor, I also served the Spanish-speaking population, many of whom were used as drug mules. I learned about their diverse cultures and countries of origin, which included Colombia, Cuba, the Dominican Republic, and Puerto Rico.

In 1991, I graduated from Fordham University with a Master's degree in Social Work, dedicated to my father's memory. The following year, my husband and I were blessed with a son, Edward Anthony Guity. We balanced family life with our careers and real estate investments, eventually moving to a countryside estate known as Oblong Farm, which had peach trees and apple orchards. Though our family was initially unenthusiastic, I felt at home surrounded by nature's tranquility.

After graduation, I passed my licensing exam and applied for a social worker position with the State of New York. While waiting for acceptance, I continued my role at Bedford Hills, providing counseling and support to the inmates. My work there was deeply fulfilling, allowing me to help women navigate their struggles and prepare for reintegration into society.

In 1995, Governor Pataki came to power and ordered layoffs for all non-permanent employees. I found myself unemployed and spent eight months at home with my toddler. During this time, I met other stay-at-home moms at the park, and my son played with their children. Although I enjoyed this time, I realized I missed working.

I searched for employment, sending resumes and looking through the New York Times. One day, I took my son in a stroller and traveled to Lincoln Hospital in the Bronx. The hospital staff cared for my son while I toured the emergency room, observing doctors and nurses in action. During my interview with the Social Work Administrator, I was offered a position as a supervisor in the Emergency Room area from 3 PM to midnight, starting on October 28th.

Feeling triumphant, I returned home to our country-style community. Soon after, I received a call from a supervisor at an Alcohol and Substance Outpatient Clinic thirty minutes from my home in Connecticut. They needed a Spanish-speaking social worker. The next day, I left my son with our neighbor, Mrs. Grant, and attended the interview. I was hired immediately. I called Lincoln Hospital to thank them for the opportunity but explained I had accepted a job closer to home.

Lucia Cayetano Guity

Working at MCCA was pleasant. We had weekly meetings to discuss cases and patient treatment, and as staff, we ate lunch together every day. Some patients were referred by the court and had their driver's licenses suspended until they completed three months of counseling with good results. I provided individual, group, and family therapy. Noticing that Hispanic clients were being sent to Bridgeport, Connecticut, I proposed offering services to the local Hispanic community. The management accepted my proposal, which increased revenue. After one year, I earned a month-long vacation and returned to Guatemala to visit my mother.

During my stay in Livingston, I received a call from my husband informing me that I had been appointed to work at the Bronx Psychiatric Hospital in New York. I needed to interview the Director of Social Work, Ms. Rosalind Ross, over the phone. The interview went well, and I was given a start date. I asked for thirty days to properly terminate my current employment and prepare for the new job.

Elated, I shared the news with my mother. I felt proud to have been selected from over a thousand applicants for a job I had waited four years for. After a month in Livingston, I returned to New York. My husband and I celebrated my new employment, and I thanked him for communicating with Ms. Ross during my vacation. I worked one week at MCCA before announcing my intention to leave, writing a resignation letter expressing gratitude for the opportunity to serve the Danbury, Connecticut, community.

Despite some colleagues' disappointment, they threw me a farewell party. I was pleased that my proposal for serving the Hispanic community had made a positive impact, and I left knowing I had made a difference.

In 1997, I began working at Bronx Psychiatric Hospital as a bilingual clinical social worker. The population was diverse, including Puerto Ricans, African Americans, Irish, Garifuna from Honduras, Asians, and veterans with PTSD, bipolar disorder, suicidal tendencies, and schizophrenia. Ages ranged from 37 to 74, with the majority being males. I provided intense psychotherapy to individuals and groups and sometimes managed a program of twenty staff, attending administrative meetings weekly.

My last assignment was at the White Plains Clinic, an outpatient annex of the hospital, where I eventually retired on May 31st, 2018. My six years working in the prison system were counted towards my retirement, totaling 26 years with New York State employment, plus nine years with Dominican Sisters, one year with MCCA, and other group home services.

I was fortunate to have a supportive husband who saw my ambition and abilities. He worked as a crane operator for a major company, requiring intellect and precision. Despite our demanding jobs, we remained in constant contact and enjoyed leisure time together.

Chapter 8
Family Expedition-Pure Bliss

We traveled twice a year, visiting Norfolk, Virginia, for thirty years, enjoying amusement attractions, fishing, sailing, shopping, and dining at Fisherman's Wharf. Our son loved playing in the sand, swimming, and swinging.

Our second vacations were usually overseas. On my fiftieth birthday, we went on our first cruise on the Carnival Miracle, visiting Costa Maya, Mexico, Belize, the Cayman Islands, Ocho Rios, Jamaica, Cozumel, and the Bahamas. The experience was epic, filled with dancing and meeting jubilant people.

The following year, we embarked on another cruise, this time on the Carnival Magic. We said "sayonara" to New York, feeling liberated from the demands of work and school. My husband, our son Edward, and I were excited about this new adventure. However, our departure was delayed by two hours on the plane at JFK Airport. The anxiety started to build up, and I began to worry that this trip might not happen. I took a deep breath, closed my eyes, and tried to stay calm. I couldn't understand why passengers had to be confined to a plane for so long. Eventually, luck was on our side, and we departed without any significant issues. I said my prayers, knowing we would arrive in Barcelona in seven hours the next morning.

Edward was seated with his dad, and I found myself next to an older woman who was a native of Barcelona. We engaged in a meaningful conversation about family and children's education. She was fascinated by my son Edward, who was wearing an official Barcelona soccer team T-shirt. She shared her snack with me and mentioned that she spoke Catalán, a dialect quite different from Spanish, which made us both laugh joyfully. After an overnight sleep, we landed at Barcelona airport at 7:30 am. The airport was beautiful and modern, only two years old, as we learned from inquiries.

We stopped by a vendor's shop filled with soccer memorabilia, and Edward was thrilled to purchase a T-shirt and a soccer ball. We took pictures and then hopped into a pretty yellow taxi with black checkered designs on it, heading to the Porte Asado Pier lot "D." As we approached, we noticed the humongous ship named "MAGIC," which appeared majestic and special. This ship was going to be our home for the next 12 days, and we were excited to see what it had to offer.

After an arduous check-in process and navigating through the large ship, we enjoyed brunch on the famous "Lido Deck." Later, we checked into our balcony stateroom, freshened up, and dressed for a formal dinner. The dining room had a magnificent view of the sunset and the ocean. We were seated with a Japanese family from New Orleans—a husband, wife, and their teen daughter, who was around Edward's age. The evening was filled with meet-and-greet moments and great conversations. I was impressed by how Edward engaged in a professional discussion about engineering with the husband and demonstrated good table manners. The five-course meal was presented with five-star flair and was absolutely delicious.

Around 1:00 am, feeling restless, I decided to explore the ship. While my husband and son were sound asleep, I ventured out and found the ship quiet, with most passengers likely asleep. As I entered the elevator, I met a woman who appeared to be in her fifties. We greeted each other and she mentioned she was looking for some tea. I agreed to join her. Her name was Sue, and she was from the UK, specifically of Welsh descent.

We headed to the Lido Deck, made our tea, and sat by a booth. Our conversation was both inspirational and a bit eerie, giving me much to ponder. Sue shared that she was traveling alone, having ventured out from her small Welsh town where everyone knew each other. She was diabetic and no longer worked due to her disability. She vividly described walking miles in the snow to her job at a school, where she served children's food, until her doctor discovered dark spots on her toes, leading to their amputation due to poor circulation. She received four insulin shots daily and shared how, in England, severe illness meant you didn't have to work.

Sue recounted her stressful experience with delays at the airport, almost missing the ship's boarding. I recalled an announcement about several missing passengers and told her how fortunate she was to have made it, as the ship typically adhered to its schedule. After our tea, we explored the ship, reaching the 12th floor, where the golf court and basketball area were located. I told her I would bring my son there. We also saw gym equipment on the deck, Al Fresco. We decided to do a light workout. The cool breeze was refreshing as we enjoyed each other's company, feeling like kids in a playground. I pedaled on a stationary bike while Sue used a stepper, both of us staring at the dark ocean, feeling the serene breeze.

As we headed back, Sue got off on the 11th floor. We agreed to meet again at the same tea and coffee area. I returned to my stateroom, filled with a sense of peace and anticipation for the days ahead.

Our first day on the ship had been eventful, covering so much ground already. It felt like the beginning of a grand adventure. The dinner earlier played a song with the lyrics "que será, será"—"whatever will be, will be"—which resonated with my mood. I was pleased to be on this journey, ready to soak in every moment like a sponge.

The next morning, my husband and I were up very early. We headed to the Lido Deck for a quick breakfast and rushed out with cups of coffee. The ship was a mile or two from Monaco, and the silence suggested most passengers were still asleep. We made our way to the jacuzzi at the front of the ship on the twelfth floor, in the Serenity corner section, which featured enclosed canopies, circular beds, hammocks, and bubbling hot jacuzzis. I removed my cover-up and prepared to enjoy the hot, bubbling water.

As the ship approached Monaco, we admired the beautiful sight of the principality. The flickering lights on the hills resembled a Christmas village, with modern high-rises adorning the slopes. The ship was being maneuvered into position, and while soaking in the jacuzzi, I faced Monaco's splendor. It was a dramatic and breathtaking arrival, making me feel rich and wealthy. My husband and I rushed back to our stateroom, feeling jubilant and ready for our day in Monaco.

By 9:00 am, we were dressed and ready to tour Monaco and Monte Carlo, where Prince Albert reigns and lives. We planned to visit the grave site of his late parents, Prince Rainier and Princess Grace of Monaco, at a cathedral. We boarded a small trolley, paying 10 euros per person. The weather was lovely, with a blue sky and a cool breeze welcoming us to this iconic and wealthy country. The streets were spotless, and the modern architecture was impressive.

Lucia Cayetano Guity

After an uphill trolley ride, we chose to walk around a building overlooking a marina with luxurious yachts on turquoise waters. The path was filled with aromatic vegetation, including honeysuckle and jasmine, and vibrant flowers. As we walked, we noticed a black Madonna and a child statue, which resonated with me as a Garifuna woman. We continued to a round patio overlooking the Mediterranean Sea, where we met a group of teenagers visiting from Sicily. We took pictures together, and they were friendly and amusing.

We walked toward the Old City, where the simple yet elegant castle stood. A crowd had gathered for the changing of the guard ceremony, which I always find fascinating. We squeezed through the crowd to get a better view as the marching band passed by. It was an exhilarating moment to be so close to the guards in their pastel blue uniforms.

After the ceremony, my husband led me to a less crowded street with souvenir stores. We met a store owner from Chile and chatted in Spanish. I purchased T-shirts and cups with Monaco prints as souvenirs. We continued to a parked trolley that took us to other areas, passing by the elegant Casino of Monte Carlo. My husband and son got off to watch a car race while I headed back to the ship, exhausted. My husband later reported capturing great photos.

That evening, we bumped into Sue, my new acquaintance from the UK, as we entered the dining restaurant. She asked to join our table, and my husband, ever charismatic, arranged seating for her. The music in the dining area created a pleasant ambiance, and I enjoyed the relaxed elegance. I had the chef's special gourmet meal of Australian lamb with salad, young potatoes, and a delicious sauce, accompanied by a glass of Pinot Grigio.

After dinner, we strolled to the other end of the ship to watch a Broadway show featuring dramatic lighting, smoke, and special effects based on magician acts. It was a fitting show for the ship named Magic.

The next morning, we arrived at the port of Civitavecchia, Italy, en route to Rome to visit the Vatican, St. Peter's Basilica, the Trevi Fountain, and the Colosseum. Sue asked if she could join us, and my husband welcomed her warmly, saying she was part of our group now. She was pleased.

We had also befriended a family from Greece and another from Canada. We all contracted a guide named Vincenzo, who carried a long pole with a medieval scarlet bag at the tip for easy identification. We walked to the Civitavecchia train station and boarded a train to Rome, with tickets costing nine euros. The scenic ride along the Mediterranean coastline was beautiful, with palm trees and cypress evergreens.

Upon arrival in Rome, we navigated through a crowded hallway to see the Colosseum, which was under construction, limiting access to just touching the walls and taking pictures. We then followed our guide to a majestic white marble building with horse statues at each corner. After a short bus ride, we walked to the crowded Trevi Fountain, managing to take good photos and grab a slice of pizza at a small restaurant.

Before leaving, my husband and I threw pennies into the fountain, hoping for a return to Rome.

We continued to roam around Rome's streets and alleys, guided by our efficient and enthusiastic guide, Vincent, whose passion for his role was contagious. His energy inspired us to keep moving, even as our feet grew weary. The fifteen of us had bonded on the ship, and my friend Sue seemed delighted to be part of our journey. Vincent lectured us on the historical significance of the Trevi Fountain, explaining how, years ago, it was a vital source of drinking water and a symbol of wealth and fertility, especially during drought seasons. People would gather around it to collect water for their homes, turning the fountain into a social hub. His words brought back memories of my childhood in the village, where water truly was life.

As we walked the streets of Rome, the city's romantic charm enveloped us. We strolled over cobblestone paths and passed through a flower market, the "Marketa Di Flori." One block from there, we reached the famous Spanish Steps, perhaps one hundred in number, with a church perched at the top. Exhausted, we chose not to climb them, instead resting on the steps alongside many others, people-watching and soaking in the ambiance. Our son, Eddie, went off in search of an ATM in the nearby Fashion District. The area felt safe, allowing Eddie to venture out on his own for cash. Upon his return, he brought back gelato, which we eagerly devoured.

We were given thirty minutes to explore the Spanish Steps and the Fashion District. Eddie returned with gelato, and we all enjoyed the treat. Vincent then guided us to an underground train station, where we hopped on a train for a short ride. After four stops, we disembarked and walked a few blocks to the Vatican. Thanks to Vincent's expertise, we bypassed the long lines and entered the Vatican Museum. The steep stairs posed a challenge for one of our elderly friends, but my husband kindly assisted her while I busied myself taking photos of Michelangelo's famous sculptures. As we entered the Sistine Chapel and the Chapel of Judgement, the magnificent paintings on the ceiling left us in awe. The original tapestry of Michelangelo, particularly the "Resurrection of Christ," was mesmerizing; Christ's eyes seemed to follow me, creating a hauntingly realistic effect.

The Sistine Chapel was packed with people, and the heat was overwhelming. I felt faint and perspired heavily, so my husband found a narrow bench for me to sit on and catch my breath. I watched the crowd, taking photos despite the no-photography rule. Vincent continued his lecture on the meaning of the Judgement painting. The chapel, dark and solemn, added to the reverent atmosphere.

We then followed Vincent through a narrow stairway leading to St. Peter's Basilica, a VIP route not open to the general public. Inside the Basilica, we encountered the sealed "En Conclave" door, used by the archbishops every twenty-five years to vote for a new Pope. I touched the cross marking the spot, and took photos. Sue faced a brief hiccup when her sleeveless blouse was deemed inappropriate, but a group member lent her a sweater and scarf. Sue joked about being "too sexy" for the Basilica, lightening the mood.

Vincent led us to the Eucharist Church, where only pilgrims were allowed. I convinced the usher to let me in, citing my long journey. Inside, nuns and people of various ethnicities prayed solemnly. I knelt and tears flowed as I reflected on the years of watching midnight masses from the Vatican on TV. The moment was overwhelming and emotional, filling me with gratitude and a sense of accomplishment. All the pain and exhaustion vanished as I toured the Basilica, feeling as though I was walking on clouds.

After leaving the Basilica, we witnessed the Vatican guards in their striped yellow and red medieval attire, another addition to my collection of change-of-guard experiences. It was time to return to Civitavecchia and board our ship, the magnificent Magic. The train ride back was uneventful, and we arrived at our stateroom, exhausted but thrilled with our day's adventures and the souvenirs we had collected.

Our bond with our new friends, including Sue and Linda with her family, had strengthened. We freshened up, showered, and dressed for our seated dinner. Eddie hurried us, eager not to be late. We met our friends at a specialty Italian restaurant on the ship called Southern Lights. We sat facing the Mediterranean Sea, watching the sunset as the ship departed Civitavecchia. The following day was a sea day, offering us a chance to relax and perhaps enjoy breakfast in bed or on our balcony.

Saturday arrived, and we docked at the port of Naples or Napoli. During breakfast, Eddie expressed his desire to explore Naples and visit Pompeii to see the ruins of a city destroyed by a volcanic eruption. However, my husband suggested taking a ferry to the island of Capri instead, a more scenic and pleasant option. We voted, and Capri won.

As we exited the ship, a beautiful marble-floored walkway with high-end shops greeted us. One jewelry shop caught my eye with its red coral necklaces and earrings, as well as a Persian necklace and earrings. I had seen a woman wearing similar jewelry at an Italian concert led by Andrea Bocelli and had always wanted to own something like it. I made the purchase, feeling triumphant and happy.

We took the ferry to Capri, accompanied by Sue and our new acquaintances. The island was breathtaking, with its iconic rock formations, evergreen hilltops, and slopes covered in lemon groves and colorful flowers. We took a funicular to higher hilltops, where shops sold melon-sized lemons and freshly made limoncello. The atmosphere was unique and unforgettable.

Window shopping in Capri was a treat, with vendors selling spices, sweets, and various lemon-themed items. We admired high-end stores like Fendi, Gucci, and Louis Vuitton, though we only shopped with our eyes. A hotel we visited charged seven hundred euros per night, which we politely declined.

We took the funicular back to sea level, enjoying the sight of the famous rock formations and colorful fishing boats docked by the shore. We sat at a corner restaurant with al fresco dining, savoring a seafood pizza topped with calamari, octopus, mussels, clams, oysters, shrimp, and white fish. I prayed I wouldn't have an allergic reaction, carrying Benadryl just in case. The limoncello perfectly complemented the seafood dish.

Our son, Eddie, enjoyed his gelato as he explored on his own. We continued shopping, stopping at a store selling lemon-themed items. The young girl behind the counter, Christina, was cheerful and welcoming, offering us samples of various treats and drinks. My husband found meloncello, which tasted just like melon.

Feeling fortunate to have visited Capri, we headed back to the dock. Sue pulled me into a shop and insisted I pick something out. I chose a scarf, making her happy. We boarded the ferry back to Naples, our hearts full of the day's experiences and the beauty of Capri.

Monday, our ship, Magic, arrived at the Port of Dubrovnik in Croatia. My husband woke me and said, "Come to the balcony. I have something to show you." I witnessed an amazing sight, reminiscent of my childhood. As the ship approached Dubrovnik, several dolphins were swimming side by side a few yards from the ship. It was very impressive. I shouted, "Thank you for coming out to greet us!" Croatia has the most beautiful sights. It is a country with thousands of small islands, some inhabited and others not. Croatia is also known for its pristine, clear waters of the Adriatic Sea. Just marvelous.

My friend Sue and I agreed to visit an island. My son would go biking with his dad up the hill. The climate was gloomy and cold as we headed toward the dock and mounted a pirate ship with a very distinguished look as though it belonged in a museum. It was very chilly; good thing we had sweaters and summer scarves. We sailed through the Adriatic seashores, with their high cliffs of yellow and red rocky clay and spiky rocks. The sea waves were hitting and smashing against these rock formations, an unusual sight. This turned out to be a rocky sail.

We finally arrived at the island. It was a very scenic place, somewhat gloomy due to its misty atmosphere and tall vegetation like eucalyptus trees and gigantic agave plants. The rows of rosemary and lavender low-ground gardens gave the entire island an exquisite aroma reminiscent of homely times of romance. Currently, the island is not inhabited, although a medium-sized castle is visible at a distance. Apparently, an aristocrat built the castle for his wife. Later, it was also occupied by monks. The irony is that these monks' things were removed (cut out) to keep them in silence.

History also indicates that the island is haunted. I was impressed by the stillness, and all we could hear was the birds chirping, the sound of peacocks, and the sight of colorful feathers. The females, however, were small, plain brown, and smaller. The aroma of honey lingered with rosemary and lavender as we proceeded with the tour. We walked over to see the cliffs. The sight was enchanting. One could hear the sea waves crashing against the rock formations. My wish was to just sit by these cliffs, admiring the crystal-clear waters of the Adriatic Sea. Then, the thought of the island being haunted freaked me out. I drew closer to my friend Sue, and we just proceeded to take photos of the gardens.

Eventually, we headed back toward the pirate ship and returned to the walled city of Dubrovnik. Sue and I enjoyed the pebble cobblestone walkways and side streets. We enjoyed some window shopping and selecting souvenirs. Later, we found a nice restaurant by an alleyway. We sat there to rest and ordered grilled snapper with salad and steamed vegetables, and the freshest bread ever—it was still warm with an exquisite aroma, reminiscent of home-baked bread with butter. This concluded our experience in Dubrovnik. We returned to the mother ship, the Magic. That evening, as the

Magic sailed away, I cried. My husband asked me why I was crying. I said, "I fell in love with Croatia." A woman on the balcony next to us was also crying. It was about the serenity, aromas, and the beautiful Adriatic Sea with its clear turquoise waters. That freshly baked bread will linger forever in my memories.

There was still more to come tomorrow when we arrived in Venice, Italy. The entrance to Venice was a sight to see. Entering the canal was spectacular. We all rushed to the front of the ship, where the majority of the people gathered, mesmerized by the sight. The ship arrived by one or two P.M., and we would be docked in Venice for two days—how wonderful. We visited the Murano Island, where we observed how the beautiful art of figurines and vases are made from sand. We watched how it is transformed in the forno. It was very hot in there, with the bright red flames melting the sand and the artist blowing into the long stick vessel while rotating it to form whatever creation they desired, adding drips of color, etc.

We purchased a few small items due to the delicate nature of these items and their high cost. We continued to walk over bridges, taking photos of the canals, and boarded the ferry boat back to the large island to visit St. Mark's Square. As we approached St. Mark's Square, one could feel and see the Venice flair, with the gondolas and bandoleros in their hats and blue and white striped t-shirts. We purchased a couple of these striped t-shirts with "Venezia" labels on them. The square was crowded, and flocks of pigeons provided entertainment to tourists as they were fed. My husband went to rest at a corner park. As we sat on the bench looking around at the greenery and colorful fuchsias, I experienced an inner feeling of love. Yes, I experienced a serene ecstasy. I asked my husband if he felt something. He said yes.

We continued to walk through narrow alleyways displaying diverse shops. My eyes caught the attention of a Murano glass blue pendant encircled with 18k gold. This jewelry has become part of my collection—I just love it.

We returned to the mother ship to eat and freshen up. By six P.M., we were out—my husband, Sue, and I. As we were walking on the dock, we noticed our son looking exhausted. He said he missed his ferry boat and walked from St. Mark's Square. I asked how. He said he bought a map and crossed many bridges, going through narrow walkways around buildings. He met lots of nice people along the way and purchased some t-shirts and souvenirs. He was ordered in to go freshen up and eat. He said he would go with us. My husband, Sue, and I took a water taxi to St. Mark's Square. We remained there until nine at night and experienced Venice at night. It was very festive. The fancy restaurants displayed white linen-covered tables al fresco. Merchants were selling trinkets that were launched up into the air, showcasing flickering lights that made the night so beautiful. We continued to stroll around among the multitude of people. It was a trio—my husband in the middle and Sue and I on either side of him. I call this experience "Venice at Night."

This is why I enjoy cruising. It allows you to visit several countries in twelve or fourteen days, experiencing the presence and special moments of adventure and newness for the mind. We met new friends, like my friend Sue, who was traveling solo but took a risk and asked us, "Can I tag along with you?" Together, we created memorable experiences of finesse, bliss, and the epitome of wealth and richness. I will end this note here; however, the trip is not over. We will return to Civitavecchia, Italy, our final destination.

I must say, however, that our leisure experiences continued after this voyage. We did a transatlantic voyage from New York City to Barcelona. We returned to Rome for eight days, residing in the Fashion District. We managed to finally reach the church on the Spanish Steps. From Italy, we traveled to Milan and took the train to Switzerland. Our lives were enriched by our adventurous spirit.

In 2019, we took our second transatlantic voyage for 29 days. This voyage took us to Bermuda, Ponta Delgada Azores, Portugal, Cádiz, Spain, Palma de Mallorca, Cannes, France, Greece, Mykonos, Santorini, Pisa, Montenegro, back to Rome and the Vatican, Sicily, Taormina, Paris, France, Cape Town, South Africa, Madagascar, Seychelles, Muscat, Oman, Saudi Arabia, and Abu Dhabi and Dubai.

Each of these countries provided different cultural experiences and presences that enriched our lives, and it would be too long to walk you through them at this time. Perhaps on another occasion, I will.

I believe that life is for the living, and if you have the opportunity and an adventurous spirit, you can enjoy the pleasures of life through these experiences.

Chapter 9
A Year Of Trials

The year 2020 will forever be etched in our memories as the time when the world came to a standstill due to the COVID-19 pandemic. It was a period marked by uncertainty, fear, and profound change. For my husband, Edward Guity, and me, it was a year that tested our resilience and brought new challenges and unexpected transformations.

When the pandemic hit, Edward decided to join the Cancer Research Foundation for Children. He vowed to become a cyclist to raise funds for this noble cause. His rationale was that with the pandemic and borders closed, he would maintain his physical health and protect himself from the virus while supporting children battling cancer. Every morning, he would cycle for four hours through the Hudson Valley Mountain trails, just twenty-five minutes from our home.

Edward's dedication to cycling was unwavering, but when he bought me a bike, I quickly realized I couldn't keep up with him. Instead, I turned my attention to cultivating a vegetable garden, a rose garden, and an herbal garden filled with oregano, thyme, lemongrass, chamomile, chives, garlic, leeks, sage, mint, ruda, holy basil, lavender, and rosemary. Creating my own little paradise helped me maintain inner calmness throughout the pandemic.

In March 2020, I felt an urge to revisit familiar places. Edward and I decided to take a trip to Lake George, only to find it desolate and eerily empty. The once-bustling hotels, restaurants, and attractions were shut down. The sight was resonant of a post-apocalyptic scene, with no motorists in sight.

Our craving for Peking duck led us to New York City's Chinatown on a Saturday, only to find it equally deserted. The streets of Manhattan, usually teeming with life, were silent, with only one or two cars passing by. The store we frequented was closed, and we returned home, deeply saddened by the stark reality of the pandemic.

Edward continued his cycling activities daily until September. His dedication to the Cancer Research Foundation culminated in his photograph being displayed on a Times Square billboard, holding his bike with one arm raised and wearing his green head cover. I took that picture of him, capturing a moment of pride and accomplishment.

However, in October, Edward's health took a sudden turn. He stopped cycling, and I grew concerned. I suggested that he continue cycling for one hour, then reduce it to half an hour, and eventually transition to walks. He did not follow through with my suggestions, of course. Edward, the most charismatic and sociable person I knew, was deeply affected by the pandemic lockdown. Unable to meet up with friends and relatives, he became anxious and restless.

To help him cope, I invited him to assist me in the garden. He began to enjoy seeing the vegetables grow from tiny two-leaf seedlings to full eggplants and tomatoes. This simple activity brought a smile back to his face.

Edward also started a radio station, playing music at people's requests and dedicating songs to me, his wife, as we sat on the deck for evening dinners al fresco. These small moments of joy helped mitigate the anxiety and isolation he felt during the lockdown.

On October 9th, 2020, Edward's legs became paralyzed, and he was rushed to the hospital. Due to pandemic restrictions, I wasn't allowed inside. He called me at 3 am, relieved to learn he didn't have COVID-19. Despite this, his condition worsened. On October 14th, 2020, at 5 am, Edward passed away due to cardiac arrest caused by Guillain-Barré Syndrome, a paralyzing condition. I administered CPR until the paramedics arrived, but he was gone.

Edward's passing was devastating. Our son, who was on a Navy mission, managed to return home in two days. It was the saddest moment of our lives. Despite the pandemic, our family and friends rallied around me. My brother Fred offered to move in with me, but I chose to cope with my grief alone.

In memory of Edward, I rented a large tent and set it up on our one-and-a-half-acre property. I hired a catering service with chefs to assist, ensuring that my beloved was sent off just as he would have liked. Despite not being wealthy, we lived a fairy tale life, rich in spirit and love. Edward Guity Sr. died so others could live, completing his mission in life. He was the most generous and friendly Garifuna man. We lived to keep each other happy, and our son is our sunshine and reason for living. Though Edward is no longer physically present, his love and soul will live eternally.

The triggers of our shared life were everywhere. I remember going to Costco once, where I struggled to lift a box of mineral water. I broke down, remembering how my man used to do all the heavy lifting for me. The mere thought of being without him by my side still sinks my heart. However, I learned to ask for help and embraced the support of my community.

The year 2020 brought immense challenges and sorrow, but it also taught me the power of resilience and the importance of cherishing every moment with loved ones because we don't know when it will become just a memory. As I continue my journey without Edward by my side, I carry his love and spirit with me, knowing that he will always be a part of me.

Lucia Cayetano Guity

Chapter 10
Finding Light In The Darkness

As my birthday drew near, I felt a strong urge to break away from the sadness that enveloped me. I couldn't bear the thought of spending it at home, surrounded by memories of Edward. So, I made a bold decision—I would travel to Belize for six weeks.

In Belize, the beauty of nature surrounded me. Snorkeling among sharks and turtles was a thrilling experience. The vibrant marine life reminded me that life goes on and there is still so much to see and explore in this world. I met new people who shared their stories of loss and healing, and I found solace in their understanding and support.

Joining widows' groups on social media was another step in my healing journey. Connecting with others who were going through similar experiences made me feel less alone. We shared our stories, our pain, and our hopes for the future. These groups became a source of comfort and strength for me.

Continuing to travel became my way of coping with my grief. Each journey brought new experiences and taught me valuable lessons. I learned to navigate new places and systems on my own, relying on my own judgment and intuition. I discovered that Edward's spirit and God's presence were always with me, guiding me and keeping me safe.

When I returned from my travels, I decided to turn my passion for travel into a business. I launched Garifuna Travel Journey LLC, where I shared my travel experiences through consulting, blogging, and digital production. I wanted to inspire others to travel and explore the world, just as I had done.

I also began working on a novel that would introduce the world to the Garifuna culture. This culture, with its resilience, self-efficiency, and self-reliance, mirrors my own journey of healing and growth. Through my writing, I hoped to honor Edward's legacy and share the beauty of my heritage with others.

The year 2020 was a year of profound loss and unexpected growth for me. It taught me that even in the darkest moments, there is always a path to healing and renewal. I emerged from that year stronger and more determined to live my life to the fullest, honoring Edward's memory every step of the way.

In April 2024, I returned to Guatemala after 24 years since my mother's death.

My reason to return was on account of two dreams I had where my father was communicating to me to go to Livingston to see my land. I began to make arrangements, packed a light suitcase, and purchased tickets. With much difficulty maneuvering arrangements to get to the airport, I managed to arrive in Guatemala City at midnight. I chose to stay at the airport until dawn. I took a taxi to the bus company that offered modern efficiency and air conditioning. The seven-hour ride was excruciating on account of an accident on the road—A tractor-trailer rolled over and caused a delay of 3 hours. With snacks, bottled water, and comfortable accommodation, I was fine. The scenic view from the window was not much appealing. Everything looked dry and weary. No sign of green vegetation; perhaps it is dry season at this time.

After seven hours I was pleased to have some familiarity to a turn. I remember a Shell gas station to the right. I said to myself, "This is Puerto Barrios." However, to my surprise, it looked trashy and unappealing but I tried to have compassion. I was here to get on a boat to Labuga Livingston. At the bus stop, I hopped into a taxi and asked to be taken to the port's Dock. The heat, as typical to Puerto Barrios, was excruciatingly hot, musty, and dusty. I managed to hire a private motor boat that would take 35 minutes to Livingston.

My husband and his grandmother helped raise Osvaldo when he was a child. I found him on FB and notified him of my arrival. The sail to Labuga was very nostalgic. It felt unreal to be en route to my place of birth, where the Rio Dulce meets the Carribean Sea. Much has changed. There were hotels and beautiful homes to the left. What used to be just mangrove and tropical vegetation now looked like Italian villas overlooking the sea, but it was still so beautiful. As my boat ride approached the famous Labuga Pier Dock, people were standing around to welcome visitors, and tuk-tuk vehicles lined up waiting for passengers. It was my first experience seeing these vehicles in Labuga. Time has really changed. Gone are the days of wooden carts tugged by an elderly man trying to earn a few bucks. I noticed Osvaldo with a grin of smile waving at me. He was very happy to see me for the first time. He arranged for a tuk-tuk ride. I told him I was very hungry. He said that his sister owned a restaurant, and she could prepare some seafood for me. He told he goes fishing early in the morning when it is still dark. He ordered the driver to take me to see my family home in Barrio Barrique. I was saddened by the sight of the house's two-story, run-down, dilapidated condition and noticed clothes hanging to dry. Squatters had taken over and didn't even cut the grass. I could not see myself living there under those conditions.

We returned to the restaurant, where I was introduced to his family. They were familiar with my late husband and welcomed me as their own. I ate fish with frita, a Garifuna meal. The atmosphere was pleasant, sitting al fresco, facing the street, and people watching while enjoying the meal with some white wine. I was grateful for this friendship because I no longer had anyone there. All the people I asked of were gone, deceased. One cousin from my village, Fella, passed away three weeks ago. Her daughter was still alive but not in good condition, as they informed me. These people who welcomed me were little children I saw the last time I was there. They were now grandparents. It gave me an eerie feeling.

Labuga was overpopulated with people from different countries: Honduras, Belize, El Salvador, and European tourists who settled there. Some indigenous people from high-in-land Alta Veracruz sought asylum from persecution also settled in Labuga for safety. There were many cars, delivery trucks, and motorcycles. There were also beautiful massive houses made of concrete in admirable designs. The Gárifuna people are effortlessly thriving to sustain themselves.

I can't expect for a town to remain the same. It is part of evolution. There were fast food and pastries restaurants on every corner, and people there were doing whatever they needed to survive.

I enjoyed my meal and Osvaldo's family hospitality. They were well compensated for their service, of course. In the GARIFUNA, we value the saying " Ou bu. Buguya Nu," which means, 'I for you and you for me. We are one.'

That Monday, Osvaldo accompanied me to see a Lawyer who was related to him to discuss the land situation. He said that a developer put a bid on the property. Papers were falsified, and the process did not go through because there were original titles with my name that carried more weight. There was also a testament written by my mother for me.

I managed to enjoy myself while in this tropical paradise. Osvaldo's sister prepared a special GARIFUNA meal for me, *Hudutu*. I helped with the preparation in the kitchen, grating coconut to extract the milk and preparing a soup concoction with fish, basil, onions, and salt for taste. Someone mashed the green and yellow plantain to dip into the soup. The meal was delicious. The hospitality I received from Osvaldo's family will always be appreciated. That night, Osvaldo and his wife invited me to "Ludy Barana," the Sea Shore Club, and we danced the night away.

Once the land issue was cleared, I chose to plan a venture into other parts of Guatemala. I hired a guide, Osvaldo, along with a driver. We headed to Antigua, Guatemala, Hanapachel, and the Majestic Water Volcano or Volcan De Agua, including the famous Lake Atitlan which was formed 2800 years ago when the Water Volcano erupted. It is said that divers have found remnants of towns under the lake's waters. The indigenous people in the area consider it sacred and mystical. We took a private boat during our stay by the lake to visit one of five towns, San Jose.

The boat ride was magical. I sprinkled myself with water as the boat splashed and bounced while crossing the lake for

35 minutes. The view of the Volcano was epic; I had to pinch myself to believe it was real. While in San Jose Town or village, we took classes on textile making and cacao production and purchased organically grown coffee produced by families on their small farms, hand-picked and unprocessed.

I would return again to stay for one week. The environment is colorful and inexpensive, and the people are pleasant and hospitable.

As a Garifuna woman who is passionate about travel, I see life as a journey filled with fulfillment and purpose.

In conclusion, my life has not been a bed of roses, but I managed to plant and establish my own rose garden that has flourished for over thirty years. It is about enjoying the moment and experiencing presence.

It is about knowing who you are. As life evolves, one builds their own values and principles based on whatever works for them. Our past values and principles influence our present, and there needs to be a balance.

In the midst of technology, poor management of land rights, fraudulence, and immorality on the rise, the Gatifuna spirituality reigns through their ancestral whispers.

My life journey has thrown jabs at me, but I remain resilient. I bounce back by turning the negative aspect of my journey into positivity triumphantly. Set time for leisure and enjoy time with family, friends, and neighbors.

Some highlights of my travel journey through life is having my son Edward Jr., and the love and appreciation of my husband, who believed in and supported my journey ventures. I've been fortunate to have crossed paths with very loving and compassionate human beings, and pleased to have made a difference in people's lives for the betterment of society.

The highlight of my travel journey was touching the ground in the Motherland in Capetown, South Africa, in 2023. Secondly, to come face to face with the Water Volcano in

Guatemala and sailed in the waters of Lake Atitlan. Thirdly, the icing on the cake was having tea at the Al-Burj-Arab Hotel in Dubai. I felt as though I died and went to heaven and came back to share my experience with the world. The food was exquisite, and the treatment Divine suited for royalty.

In completing my book on *GARIFUNA travel journey, Labuga Livingston is phenomenal.* It helped me heal grief from many losses. I feel that people are born to complete their mission in life.

I enjoyed writing the historical perspective of me and my Garifuna culture, demonstrating how I evolved by beating odds and obstacles with compassion and love.

I hope you find it inspirational and empowering.

With much gratitude, I thank you.